READ ME
AT SCHOOL

Ne

by Morgan is Editorial Director of the Macmillan
Children's Books poetry list. She has edited a number
of bestselling anthologies, including *Read Me and
Laugh* and *Christmas Poems*. She lives in Hampshire
with her husband, two children and two cats called
Angel and Cosmo.

A Poem About School for Every Day of the Year

Chosen by Gaby Morgan

MACMILLAN CHILDREN'S BOOKS

This book is dedicated to all the staff and pupils of
Shottermill Infant School, Surrey. An outstanding school.
Special thanks to Cathy Cooke and Vanessa Vian.

And for Shirley Lewis, Louise Trant, Michele Andjel,
Rachel Petty, Rebecca McNally, Lyn Weston and
Sue and Peter Morgan. See me after class!

First published 2009 by Macmillan Children's Books
a division of Macmillan Publishers Limited
20 New Wharf Road, London N1 9RR
Basingstoke and Oxford
Associated companies throughout the world
www.panmacmillan.com

ISBN 978-0-330-47209-8

1 3 5 7 9 8 6 4 2

A CIP catalogue record for this book is available from
the British Library.

Typeset by Intype Libra Limited
Printed and bound in the UK by CPI Mackays, Chatham ME5 8TD

Contents

January

February

March

April

May

June

July

August

September

October

November

December

January

Whizz Kid

Beth's the best at reading,
Gary's good at sums,
Kirsty's quick at counting
on her fingers and her thumbs,
Wayne's all right at writing,
Charles has lots of chums,
but I'm the fastest out of school
when home time comes.

Gina Douthwaite

Watching

Snowflakes fall like friends.

Not cold inside my head
but warm
soft and gentle;
not bullying
not shouting
not pulling me this way and that.

But laughing
whispering
sharing gossip
having fun.
They are all around
like a playground full of happiness.

They wrap me
touch me with kindness
make me feel good somehow.

Patricia Leighton

Winter Morning: Winter Night

This morning I walked to school
through the dark
it was so cold my shadow shivered
under the street lamps.

My feet cracked the ice
that glittered as hard as the frosted stars
stuck on the sky's blue back.

Cars crept by like giant cats
their bright eyes shining.

Tonight I walked over the snow
the moon's cool searchlight
splashed its glow over the garden

Picking out details of rooftops and hedges
as clearly and sharply
as a summer stillness just after dawn.

Cars on the street roared like lions
bounding over the wet tarmac.

David Harmer

How Teachers Leave
School Each Evening

The dance teacher floats down the stairway
and waltzes herself to the door.
Behind her the maths teacher counts every step
as he paces across the floor.

The geography teacher struggles to find
a different route home each night.
The PE teacher sets new daily records
for the swiftest homeward flight.

The English teacher recites to himself
lines of poetry by Keats.
The drama teacher's on camera,
a movie star in the streets.

The RE teacher prays
that there'll be no traffic queues.
The physics teacher knows there will
and regularly blows a fuse.

The IT teacher imagines he's left
as he follows some virtual route on screen.
It's a mystery why the history teacher
is met each night by a limousine.

Our music teacher, an Elvis freak,
plays air guitar along the drive.
With his rocker's quiff and Las Vegas suit
he's out there somewhere perfecting his jive.

But the teacher who's young and still keen
reluctantly closes the door,
ticks off the hours and minutes till she can be
back with her class once more.

Brian Moses

Day Closure

We had a day closure on Monday
and I spent the morning in bed,
but the teachers went in as usual
and someone taught them instead.

And I thought of them all in the classroom,
stuck to their seats in rows,
some of them sucking pen lids.
Head Teacher scratching his nose.

Perhaps it's a bit like an MOT
to check if teachers still know
the dates of our kings and queens
or the capital of so and so.

Perhaps they had tables and spellings,
did the Head give them marks out of ten?
And then, if they got any wrong,
did he make them learn them again?

I thought of them out at break time
playing football or kiss chase or tag,
picking up teams in the playground
or scoffing crisps from a bag.

If I'd been a fly on the wall,
I might have watched while they slaved,
I'd have seen who asked silly questions
Or if anyone misbehaved.

I thought of them all going home,
crossing the road to their mums.
They looked very grim the next day.
It couldn't have been much fun.

Brian Moses

The Trees Behind the Teachers' Cars
First day back after Christmas

The trees have turned into wicked old witches,
clawing at the mist with gnarled fingers,
weaving white webs round their black broomstick hair,
to trap any teacher who lingers.

Kate Williams

New Year Resolution

Snowballs hurt,
when bigger children throw them,
hard.
Spring term just begun
and play time didn't seem much fun.

I hid, from everyone, behind a tree;
stood there, shivering,
small, so lonely.

Only little me,
with a robin for company,
in that great world
of swirling flakes.

What minute marks a robin makes;
inside my footprint, tiny traces.

I glanced at him, he glanced at me,
tilting his face, as if to say,
'Hey, you're not so small, after all.'

I started back,

walking tall,

shaping a snowball.

Mike Johnson

Assembly

I don't want to see any racing in the corridor,
a gentle glide's what we expect in here;
not that I mind a little heavy-handed fear
but you high spirits must slow down.

And I've had complaints that some of you
slip out at playtime. Let it be quite clear
that you stay in the graveyard till you hear
the bell. The chippy's out of bounds,
so is the sweetshop and your other favourite haunts.
I'll stop your little fun and groans:
there'll be a year's detention in the dungeons
for anyone caught chewing anything but bones.

And we'll have no more silly tricks with slamming doors,
at your age you should be walking through the walls.
And it isn't nice to use your loose heads as footballs
or vanish when you're being spoken to.

And finally, I really must remind you
that moans are not allowed before midnight,
especially near the staffroom. It's impolite
and disturbs the creatures – I mean teachers –
resting in despair and mournful gloom.
You there – stop wriggling in your coffin, I can't
bear to see a scruffy ghost –
put your face back where it was this instant
or you won't get to go howling at the moon.

Class Three, instead of double Shrieking
you'll do Terminal Disease with Dr Cyst;
Class Two stays here for Creepy Sneaking.
The rest of you can go. School dismissed.

Dave Calder

At the End of School Assembly

Miss Sparrow's lot flew out,
Mrs Steed's lot galloped out,
Mr Bull's lot got herded out,
Mrs Bumble's lot buzzed out.

Miss Rose's class . . . rose,
Mr Beetle's class . . . beetled off,
Miss Storm's class thundered out,
Mrs Frisby's class whirled across the hall.

Mr Train's lot made tracks,
Miss Ferry's lot sailed off,
Mr Roller's lot got their skates on,
Mrs Street's lot got stuck halfway across.

Mr Idle's class just couldn't be bothered,
Mrs Barrow's class were wheeled out,
Miss Stretcher's class were carried out
And
Mrs Brook's class
Simply
        trickled
                away.

Simon Pitt

Story Time

Handfuls of rusty leaves are flung
Against the library window
'Once upon a time, long, long ago'
There is a tugging at the door
'Upon a hillside in a granite tower'
It howls along the corridor and stairs
We snuggle deeper into chairs
'There lived a boy whose eyes were like a storm at sea'.
It suddenly seems darker than an afternoon should be.

Petonelle Archer

My Lunch

I didn't like my lunch today
and traded it for Amy's.
Amy didn't like it so
she traded it for Jamie's.
Jamie didn't like it so
he traded it with Brian.
Brian didn't like it so
he traded it with Ryan.
Ryan didn't like it so
he traded it with Jack.
Jack just traded it for mine
and now I've got it back.

Linda Knaus

The Schoolkids' Rap

Miss was at the blackboard writing with the chalk,
When suddenly she stopped in the middle of her talk.
She snapped her fingers – snap! snap! snap!
Pay attention children and I'll teach you how to rap.

She picked up a pencil, she started to tap.
All together children, now clap! clap! clap!
Just get the rhythm, just get the beat.
Drum it with your fingers, stamp it with your feet.

That's right, children, keep in time.
Now we've got the rhythm, all we need is the rhyme.
This school is cool, Miss Grace is ace.
Strut your stuff with a smile on your face.

Snap those fingers, tap those toes.
Do it like they do it in the video shows.
Flap it! Slap it! Clap! Snap! Clap!
Let's all do the schoolkids' rap!

John Foster

The Staff

Miss Linnet is neat and very precise
She flutters her skirts around.
She sweeps along the corridors
thin fingers curled round
her art pad, feet tapping along
in stiletto heels, sharp as tacks.

Mrs Tabby has green eyes.
Be sure they'll find you out.
You may think she is snoozing
Curled up in her chair
but one ear is always pricked
to see what you're doing there.

Mr Mastiff's our head.
He's gruff and snappy.
Miss Linnet and Mrs Tabby say
his bark's as bad as his bite.
You'll never get the better of him –
he's always in the right.

Angela Topping

Black Board

I was sitting in the classroom
waiting for the teacher to come,
I saw words scribbled on the board.
Some were complete,
in fragments were some.

I stared at the board,
at the scribbles' clauses,
which slowly fade away
as time passes.

I looked on and on
to find some letters,
known words they had formed once
but now what matters?
I sailed away in my thoughts,
As if I was on a ship, aboard . . .
Memories flashed by,
Just like the scribbles on the board.

Nivedita Bhattacharjee

The Fairy School under the Loch
(Sgoil a'Morghain, Barra, The Hebrides)

The wind sings its gusty song.
The bell rings its rusty ring.
The underwater fairy children
dive and swim through school gates.
They do not get wet.

The waves flick their flashing spray.
A school of fish wriggles its scaly way.
The underwater fairy children
learn their liquidy lessons.
Their reading books are always dry.

The seals straighten in a stretchy mass.
Teresa the Teacher flits and floats from class to class.
The underwater fairy children
count, play, sing and recite,
their clothes not in the least bit damp.

The rocks creak in their cracking skin.
A fairy boat drifts into a loch of time.
The underwater fairy children
lived, learned and left this life –
their salty stories now dry as their cracked wings.

John Rice

Front of the Class

I sit at the front of the class
and try to get on with my work.
The back row are mucking about.

Tom's had a paper dart flown at his head,
it's caught in his hair
and he doesn't know it's stuck there.

He looks like a scoop of ice cream
with one of those horrible fan-shaped biscuits
sticking out the side of it.

I want to laugh out loud
but I suppose I mustn't.
I always have to do the right thing.

Often, when I shouldn't, I just want to be silly,
stop being old Serious Drearious,
or Sternly Burnley – and just be me.

I'm back row material, really I am.
I could mess about with the worst of you,
have a laugh, see the silly side of everything.

It's what I'm like on the inside.
But on the outside it's just not that easy
when you're the teacher.

Trevor Parsons

Cats Rule, OK?

A sleek black cat,
Haughty, cool,
Regularly
Prowls the school.

Prowls the classrooms,
Corridors,
Ghosts through windows –
And through doors.

Gains the roof:
Surveys below,
At break,
The playground rodeo.

Soon, leaving fights
And games and chat,
Everyone
Observes the cat.

'Must have got up there
For the view'.
'How'll he get down?'
'I've not a clue!'

Without so much as
Just Watch Me,
Cat leaps down:
Lands perfectly.

Saunters off
On velvet paws –
To considerable
Applause.

Glances back
As if to say:
Here at school
Cats Rule, OK?

Eric Finney

School Yard in the Snow

Silent,
in this often noisy place,
I stand and stare
in wonder

At snow,
the first
I've ever seen.

A crisp white duvet,
pulled across our school yard,
while the world was sleeping.

Concrete lost in diamonds,
sudden magic fallen,
from a frozen winter sky.

I feel happy, so I sing:
'In the bleak mid School Yard!'
(But it's not bleak really, it's brilliant!)

White waves lapping red brick walls.
Icicles dancing on the cross-wire fence.

Everything's different today.
Fresh and new and amazing.
Snow . . . I love it!

I walk in gentle circles.
Softly . . . slowly . . .

Crunch!

I like
the way it sounds,
the way it feels.

I'm an explorer,
the first to see
this silent place,
this special place,
our school yard
in the snow.

Tony Norman

Miss

Please, Miss, my mother, Miss,
I've come to tell you this, Miss,
I, Miss, won't, Miss,
Be at school tomorrow, Miss.

Anon.

The Escape

The teacher is droning,
boring the class.
Eyes have gone glassy
as words skitter past,
mouths have dropped open
as daydreams take hold
and children go hunting
for ill-gotten gold,
children go riding on

fairground attractions
or skydiving, speed boating,
seeing some action.
They are zooming through Space,
they are pirates on ships
or are down at the beach
eating fried fish and chips.
They are stars of the screen
or heroes of sport
or flaunting the cool, trendy
clothes that they've bought.
The voice of their teacher
drones on and on
but nobody's listening,
everyone's gone.

Marian Swinger

Madcap Days

On windy playtimes
titchy infants go berserk,
dash round in circles
in and out of climbing frames,
jump up and over
stepping blocks
yelping like wild cubs.

In the junior playground
boys zoom around,
hands in pockets,
anoraks spread wide,
pretending to be Draculas
or hell bent Skywalkers
on raiding patrols.

Girls scatter like mad leaves,
start games of tig-and-catch;
scream, shriek, shout,
pull hair, arms, coats;
twizzle until they are giddy,
play drunk and wrap themselves
round netball posts.

In the staffroom
teachers hug mugs
of tea and coffee,
gaze through the window
and sigh.
'High as kites,' they mutter, 'high as kites.
Roll on the home time bell.'

Patricia Leighton

Routes
1 The Walk to School

Down Barking-dog Lane
past the street with the boat
   Clouds rush by
   Sometimes it rains

Up Old-lady-waving Road
past the field with the car
   Clouds hang still
   Aeroplanes drone

Down Skateboard Steps
past the shop with the cat
   Clouds make shapes
   Reflect in windowpanes

2 *The Drive to School*

radio shouts
Mum shouts
belt tight
window steam
Dad shouts
radio shouts
feel hot
feel sick
radio, Mum,
Dad shout
shout shout
every day
same shout
same hot
same sick
same same
same same

Ian McMillan

Playtime Footy

It's a game of three halves at our school,
Morning break, lunch and afternoon play.
Down with the sports bag posts,
Thirteen a side and first to thirty wins.

In Summer it's a game of four halves.
You've got to get there early,
Half eight at the very latest
Or else you don't get on the team you want.

Three halves or four,
Some games lasted a week
Monday to Friday
Adding up the scores.

Playground footy, a full match could be
A game of twenty halves,
At least thirteen a side
And first to fifty wins.

Paul Cookson

Our Headmaster

He ruffles your hair when you go by,
knows your name. He can sort out
any mess from sewing to sums.
He's like Superman, he can fly.
He is calm with those who shout.
He's shy of grown-up dads and mums.

Angela Topping

Changing Time

My favourite subject's Gym,
My worst is Changing.
It's a shame they go together,
That needs rearranging.

Frances Nagle

Every Night Mr Miller Dreams

Every night Mr Miller dreams
of the day he will retire.
There'll be a small party
in the staffroom
during the lunch hour
and at final assembly
he'll receive a major gift
from the whole school
plus presents
from individual pupils,
who will be heartbroken
to see him leave.
Children, past and present,
(some now grown-up)
will file past to thank him
for being so inspirational
– for changing their lives.

In the evening
a large group of colleagues and friends
will take him out for drinks
and a meal.
There will be speeches
charting his impressive career
and praising his achievements.

He can't wait.

Day two. Week one. First job.
A long way to go.

Every night Mr Miller dreams.

Bernard Young

When You Meet Your Friend

When you meet your friend,
your face brightens –
you have struck gold.

Kassia

I Hear

When I think of school I hear
High shouts tossed
like juggled balls in windy yards, and lost
in gutters, treetops, air.
And always, somewhere,
piano notes waterfall
and small sharp voices wail.
A monster-roar surges – GOAL!
The bell.

Then doors slam.
There's the kick, scuff, stamp of shoes
down corridors that trap and trail echoes.
Desk-tops thud with books, kit-bags.
A child's ghost screams as her chair's pushed back.
Laughter bubbles up and bursts.
Screech-owl whistles, quick-fox quarrel flares,
the voice barks QUIET!

All sit. All wait.
Till scraped chalk shrieks
and whispers creep.
Cough. Ruler crack. Desk creak.
And furtive into the silence comes
A tiny mouse-scrabbling of pens.
Scamper. Stop. Scamper. Stop. Tiptoe

And there, just outside the top window
as if it had never ceased to be
but only needed listening to
a scatter of birdsong, floating free.

Berlie Doherty

The New Girl

The new girl stood at Miss Moon's desk,
Her face pale as a drawing
On white paper,
Her lips coloured too heavily
With a too-dark crayon.

When the others shouted, 'Me! Me!'
I curled my fists,
Tried not to think of friendship,
Or whispered secrets,
Or games for two players.
But the empty seat beside me
Shimmered with need
And my loneliness dragged her like a magnet.

As she sat down
I caught the musty smell of old forests,
Noticed the threads that dangled
At her thin wrists,
The purple stitches that circled
Her swan's neck.
Yet I loved her quietness,
The way she held her pencil
Like a feather,
The swooping curves of her name,
The dreaminess of her cold eyes.

At night, I still wonder
Where she sleeps,
If she sleeps,
And what Miss Moon will say
To her tattered parents
On Open Day.

Clare Bevan

No Feel for Numbers

In English
I'm a livewire!
Ideas
Whizz
Fizz
Crackle
From my brain
Like fireworks at a display.
Words
Zap
Snap
Sizzle
From my nib
Like sparks from a white-hot electrode!

But in Maths
My thoughts become static
(My hair stands on end!)
And as the minutes drag by
My brain gets
Number
And
Number
And
Number
And
Number . . .

Philip Waddell

A Near Miss

As Nick boots the ball
straight at goal, his eyes say, 'YESSS!!!!!!'

The crossbar says,
'No.'

David Bateman

February

Coming Home

At twilight by the fireside
We munched hot buttered toast,
Watched pictures in the cinders,
Huddled warm and close;
While you drew me a memory
Of us walking in the rain –
Through the puddles,
Round the streets,
Till we got home again
In time to light the fire up
And pour out cups of tea,
Pull the curtains, fill a jug
With crunchy sticks of celery:

But in that crumpled drawing now
All that I can see
Is one great big umbrella (that's you)
And one pair of wellies (that's me)!

David Greygoose

School

I see the lucky river dancing away from the school that
  holds me tight.
I see the humming trees waving to the music.
I see the crows taunting me with their freedom.
I see the clouds racing from the sky and crushing the sun.
I see the computers lighting up the darkness and catching
  your eyes.

I feel the crumbling clouds, dipping and diving through the
  sky.
I feel the pummelling river crushing my legs and destroying
  everything in its path.
I feel the chilly wind, creeping into the classroom.
I feel the destroying rain laughing, as it ruins our day.
I feel the hail stones crashing onto the roof cracking the
  slates.
I feel the vines creeping up windows, pulling the glass out
  of place.

I would rather be playing rugby, running, writing.
I would rather be catching, kicking, climbing.
I would rather be laughing, lying, living.
I would rather be eating, eagerly, easily.
I would rather be tasting, teasing, twirling.

I love break time, kicking a football around the field.
I love playing 'off ground it' with my friends.
I love looking out of the window and watching the clouds
    go past.
I love going home.
I love seeing my Mum.

Oscar Dilke (11)

Stop Calling Me, Snow

Stop calling me, snow, I can't come out yet,
    I've got ten sums to do that the teacher just set.
So it's no good you flapping your lovely white wings,
    It's half an hour yet till the playtime bell rings.

Some kids will stay in, but not me – no fear!
I'll dive straight for my wellies – I can see them from here –
And I might build a snowman, or perhaps a snow queen,
    Or I might just tread prints where nobody's been.

Then an igloo maybe, with a tunnel to crawl,
Or perhaps I'll roll up a monster snowball.
I'll stand in the whirl of your flakes till I'm dizzy,
But I can't come just yet – I'm supposed to be busy . . .
There's this sum: **Find half of a half.** I don't know . . .
I simply can't think . . . stop calling me, snow!

Eric Finney

Teacher Says

Our teacher says:
Zip your lips!
Sit up straight!
Walk don't run . . .
. . . but don't be late.

Bottoms on the floor.
No wriggling about.
Speak up clearly . . .
. . . but DON'T SHOUT!

Cross your legs,
hands on head.
Don't move at all
BUT DO AS I SAID!

Michaela Morgan

Winter Playground

In the cold winter sunshine
The children stand against the wall.
They look like washing on a line,

Neat red coat, stripy mitts,
Narrow green tights with a hole in the knee.
Still and stiff, frozen in a row.

Across the playground
Three boys are chasing a ball.
A little dog barks through the fence.

A skipping rope curves –
'One I love, two I loathe . . .' –
As the girls hop and jump.

The teacher stalks, eyes darting,
Scattering marbles in his way,
Keeping a lookout for TROUBLE.

But from the train window
It's the still ones I see, the quiet ones,
Straight and stiff against the wall,
Like washing, frozen on the line.

Jennifer Curry

Ice

Shimmering, glimmering,
polished like glass,
ice patch in the playground,
thawing fast.

Slithering, gliding,
balancing tricky,
arms and legs windmill . . .
Ow! That was slippy.

Tingling, glowing,
soggy, steaming,
back in the classroom,
faces beaming.

Jane Clarke

Yuan Tan – Chinese New Year

Time now
when days are turning
from the greys of winter to
the coming spring
time now
for burning of
the kitchen gods.
Their smoke, unfurled,
will take our message
to the gods on high.

Time now for dancing.
For the Lion who will bring
good fortune. Banish
evil from the world.
Time for gifts. To light
the fireworks of hope.
To try. Look forward.
Have no fear.
This is New Year.

Ann Bonner

Make It Bigger, Eileen!

In Art I drew a park
With a pond, and railings, and children playing . . .
And trees with multi-coloured leaves
And mothers with pushchairs and wearing hats that
   jumped
And joggers running with three legs
And skaters – skating on thin ice with elephants on their
   backs
And pigeons playing cards on bread tables
And grass with eyes and noses
And flowers with walking sticks and headphones
And clouds that rained smells
And a sun as deep as an ocean
And stones that bled
And a rainbow with stairs.

Sir said . . .
'Tut, tut, tut – bigger, Eileen, your picture must be bigger'
So I drew a duck.

Joseph Coelho

9

Staff Meeting

The teachers have gathered in private to talk
About their collections of left-over chalk . . .

Bits that are rare, bits they just like,
And fragments they've saved just in case there's a strike.

One has a blue that you don't often see,
Another a remnant from nineteen-oh-three.

They've thousands of pieces in boxes and tins,
Each sorted and counted with tweezers and pins.

And, when all their best bits have been on display,
They'll take them home carefully . . . and lock them away.

Nick Toczek

History Lesson:
Part Two – The Romans

All over their Empire
the Romans built impressive buildings
such as forts, villas and monuments.
In big cities they constructed huge *Amphitheatres*
where great games and spectacles were held.

The best known of these
are the Roman Games with contests,
often to the death, between animals,
between men and between women combatants.

It was in one of these amphitheatres
that Miranda, the wife of Emperor Tiberius Tempus,
accidentally fell from her balcony into the arena
and was attacked and eaten by a tiger.

The tiger was told off and sent to bed.
Everyone agreed it was bad he ate her,
and now the Emperor was sad he ate her,
and poor old Miranda was mad he ate her,
but the tiger said she was tasty and he was
GLADIATOR!

John Rice

11

A cold is going round

A cold is going round, you see. I sneeze on Leigh, he coughs on Anne, she breathes on Yash, he holds Kim's hand, she sniffles over Magdalena, Stan, Fatima, and Irina, they sniffle, and then blow their noses on tissues that are Mrs Rose's. She sneezes over Raj and me. A cold is going round, you see.

Jane Clarke

Beware! Take Care!

Our school caretaker, Mr Mole,
Didn't take care – so he fell in a hole.
When your job is about taking care,
If there's a hole in the ground you should beware.

*(PS – Don't worry about the hole in the ground – the police
are looking into it.)*

Ian Billings

desk

It was stuffy in the classroom.
He put his hand inside his desk,
feeling for a pencil. It was cool in there,
he let his hand swing aimlessly around.
The space within seemed vast, and when
he reached in further he found

nothing, could feel no books, no ruler.
His hand floated as if in a bath of shadows,
airy and refreshing, not at all
the same place that the rest of him was in.

He put both hands in, let them drift
deeper, this way and that. It was more than empty,
the inside had no sides. His hands
never reappeared through some unexpected hole.
He lifted the lid quietly a little more. A waft
of soft air cooled his face, the same
as on summer nights or under leafy trees.

He bent his head down to the gap. He looked inside.
Dark as deep water, deep as a clear night sky.
He smiled. He put his head inside.
'What are you doing?' asked the teacher. But he didn't
   hear.
He slid his shoulders in, and then
before anyone could reach to stop him,
he bent from the waist, kicking his chair back,
and with a muffled cry of pleasure
dived. For a split second,
as the room filled with fresh air,
we watched his legs slide slowly down into the desk
and disappear. And then the lid fell back,
shut, with a soft thud.

Dave Calder

49

Love Hearts
sweets for the sweet

February 14th
playing Cupid
girl on my table acting stupid
passing sweets to me.

They say I Love You

an You're so Fine,

my friends crease up at Please Be Mine.

She must have packets of them.

All through maths they come

Great Guy   Don't Blush

Then Trust Me – that kind of mush

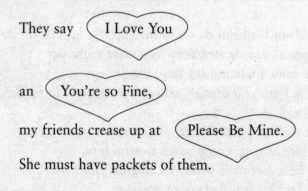

It's really getting to me.

Then (Speak to me) and (Hold Me Tight)

So at break I go up to her. All right!
She blinks at me. Her smile is growing.

Offers a sweet – (Be Kind) is showing.

I snatch them, push her, run off crowing.

All afternoon I'm thinking how she felt.
I smell the sweet and sickly scent
as pastel messages fizz and melt.

I send back (Crazy!) and (No Chance.)

I nudge and snigger (Wanna Dance?)

I chuck (No Way) and flick (Big Deal)

I throw (In Love) and make her squeal

Then,

when all my friends have gone away

I quietly give her Don't Cry

and U.R.O.K.

Michaela Morgan

15

An Average Poem

This is an average poem;
it happens to be ten lines long
and happens to consist of exactly eighty words. Count
   them!

This line contains the average number of words.

Of its words the word 'the' is the most common
appearing no fewer than five times.
This poem has fifty-six different words.
If you wanted to make bar or pie charts
using the data in this poem you could
though I wouldn't bother . . . it *is* just an average poem!

Philip Waddell

Playground Wanderer

Am I invisible?

Because
you don't seem to see
me.

Because
you don't seem to see
how I have to wander around
that playground.

Because
you don't seem to see
that every breaktime
is a lifetime
of waiting
for the bell
to ring.

But
you do know me
and by many names.

New kid.
Bright kid.
Odd kid.
Big kid.
Misfit.
Or just plain
Different.

Do you see me now?

James Carter

The Pencil Stub
for William Patten School

When I was new I drew
the leather shoe lace on a magic shoe.

You shaved me down.

I wound my lead around
the leaves of an ancient
willow tree.

You shaved me down.

I drew a circle, you
rubbed me out,
I became a careful square.

You shaved me down.

I was happiest tracing
the face of your mother –
her plaited hair,
her sparkling slate grey eyes.

And still you shaved me down.

I could still conjure the universe,
skirt Saturn with a silver ring,
chase the rain falling from
a shooting star.

Chrissie Gittins

Family

My teacher says if I don't tidy up
a drift of hogs will waddle into school
and move right in, or a rhumba of rattlesnakes
or a mischief of rats. But I don't care;
I'd rather be running with a leap of leopards
soaring with an exaltation of larks
swimming with a shiver of sharks
than be stuck inside straightening my desk.
An unkindness of ravens is calling me.
Can you hear it? We're family.

Linda Lee Welch

Books R4 Everyone

Books are for everyone
Everyone to read
To make you learn new wordz!
And mek yu knowledge increase.

Books are for everyone
From an early age.
Like books wid pictures
Mek yu wanna turn a page.

There's fiction, non-fiction, science fiction too.
History an mysteries an fantasies for you.
Inside every book
You can learn something new.

About other people and your self.
Don't let books catch dust on the shelf.
They stand so lonely in a bookcase.
Read a book and put a smile on its face.

Books will take you way back in time.
Pages and wordz from the authors mind.
How much can you take, or your imagination hold.
Some of the best books to read; are really really old.

Check out the past, check out the future.
Every book you read is another adventure.
Write your own book! On a computer.
Be a bookworm or be a book master.

Books are for everyone
Everyone to read.
To make you learn new wordz!
And mek yu knowledge increase.

Donavan Christopher

Playtime

Sliding, soaring, surging, swaying,
Squirming, steadying . . . shooting . . . scoring.

Shouting, screaming, shrieking, sneaking,
Swerving, scorching . . . spinning . . . seeking.

Squaring, straining, stepping, stretching,
Standling, shaping . . . saluting . . . soldiering.

Sickening, shivering, shuddering, sniffing,
Sobbing, sheltering . . . stroking . . . soothing.

Spoiling, scheming, summoning, spotting,
Sidling, scheming . . . sneaking . . . spying.

Fifteen minutes of fun?

Redvers Brandling

Here Lies Mad Lil

Here lies Mad Lil the dinner lady
In this spot that's cool and shady.
She used to be all rant and rave-y
Now she's buried in her grave-y.

Jan Dean

Photo Opportunity

I'm waiting in line
For the class photo
I'm getting my face ready
Trying out
A few expressions
A few good looks:
   casual
   hard
   INTERESTING
   cool
I think I'll go
For *casual-cool*
And wait for the shutter to click.
Clunk!

So
How come
When the photos come back
In their special offer pack
I look just like I did
(Just another soppy kid)
Last time?

Trevor Millum

A Wonderful Week

On Monday I'm sure I heard a dragon,
Giving a mighty roar.
Teacher said it was just the pipes,
Rumbling under the floor.
On Tuesday I'm sure I saw a witch,
Swooping across the sky.
Teacher said it was just a scrap
Of dark cloud drifting by.
On Wednesday I'm sure I whiffed a wizard,
Cooking up a spell.
Teacher said it was just the lunchtime
Stew that I could smell.
On Thursday I'm sure I saw a ghost,
Up on the bell-tower roof.
Teacher said it was just a pigeon,
Fluttering home to roost.
On Friday I sat and thought for a bit.
Teacher is probably right.
But school isn't going to be half such fun,
With nothing to give me a fright.

Julia Rawlinson

24

Girl in the Library

Pores over star maps
Like a sailor;
Behind her great iron pillars
Twist like barley sugar
To the pitched white roof
That keeps her from the sky.
Before her the staircase
Corkscrews into ground
She cannot leave.
She leafs longingly through galaxy and
        galaxy
While solid stones of all around
Slur and diffuse – unfold like petals
Or slow milk clouds in tea.
The library is melting as she reads,
Like time-lapse film of rainstorms
        clustering / blossoming
        clustering / blossoming
Space and space and million-studded space.

Jan Dean

Football in the Rain

It's drizzling.
'Football practice!'
'Oh, sir!
Do we have to?'
We look hopefully at Mr Tomkins,
But he says
'Don't be such babies!'
So out we go.

It's raining harder.
We all start to moan,
'Can't we go in, sir?
We're getting soaked!'
But Mr Tomkins is not impressed.
'Tough. Get on with it!'
He says, putting up his umbrella
And retreating to the touchline.

It's coming down in buckets.
There are puddles all over the pitch,
And the rest is just mud.
Eddy falls over,
And comes up looking like
The Mud Monster from Hell.
We all start falling over,
Because we all want to look like that.

It's really chucking it down.
Mr Tomkins gets rain in his whistle.
gurgle-gurgle-PHEEEP!
'Everybody in!'
We start moaning again.
'Oh, sir!
Do we have to?'

David Orme

Teacher's Pet

Teacher's pet isn't Billy
or Darren or Sharon or Lee
Teacher's pet isn't Sally
or Vicky or Nicky or me
Teacher's hunting for her pet
She's crawling around on all fours
Teacher's pet is a big black spider
and she keeps it in her drawers.

Roger Stevens

Absent

Dear Teacher,
my body's arrived
it sits at a table
a pen in its hand
as if it is able
to think and to act
perhaps write down the answer
to the question you've asked

but don't let that fool you.

My mind is elsewhere.
My thoughts far away.

So apologies, teacher,
I'm not here today.

Bernard Young

Roman Day

The Romans are coming –
they've breastplates and swords –
while we're just the peasants,
the British hordes.

We're dressed in sacking,
and make lots of noise
while they're wearing tunics –
even the boys.

Romans build roads
and baths and stuff,
yet one Roman day
isn't quite long enough;

but here come our Romans
(they're all in Year 5):
they're the most civilized
people alive

or so they say
as they push us about
'cos we're just the peasants –
but they should watch out.

Just look at their future.
In two thousand years
the Romans have all gone
but we are still here.

Jill Townsend

29th February

This is the rare
one in four years
twenty-five per cent
free discount
extra bonus
the not-to-be-missed
longer-than-it-seems
dream date.

So make the most of it –
you'll have to wait
one thousand
four hundred and sixty
days and nights
till it's back again,
so don't sleep through it
and don't look, just leap.

Lawrence Sail

March

Assembly

We assemble.
That's why it's called
assembly.
We sit cross-legged.
The area of the bottom
multiplied by the number of pupils
is greater than the area
of the hall floor.
We squiggle, we squeeze,
we squash, we squabble.
Jamie is asked to stay behind.
Behind is another word for bottom.
Miss walks on the stage.
So does Miss, Miss, Sir,
Miss, Sir, Miss, Miss and
Miss.
We have a talk about being good.
It is good to be good.

It is bad to be bad.
We will all be good.
We sing a song about trees.
The bone in my bottom
cuts into the floorboards.
I'm not worried about the floorboards.
Miss reads out the notices
but nobody notices.
We stand up.
I pull my bottom bone
out of the floorboards.
We line up like soldiers,
like prisoners, like refugees.
We file out
in a sensible manner.
The hall is now empty.
Except for Jamie.

Steve Turner

Bell Rings

bell rings	*you rise*
voice calls	*you eat*
radio speaks	*you walk*
bell rings	*you enter*
bell rings	*you sit*
your name is called	*you speak*
bell rings	*you move*
bell rings	*you move*
bell rings	*you eat*
bell rings	*you sit*
bell rings	*you stand*
bell rings	*you jump*
bell rings rings rings	
	you queue
voice speaks	*you nod*
voice shouts	*you eat*
radio sings	*you listen*
tv says time	*you move*
set clock	
it ticks	*you sleep*
	and dream
	you really not
	machine

Trevor Millum

Rainy Monday Morning Playtime Blues

We can draw
　　if we want to.
Cut from magazines
　　if we want to.
Do word-searches
　　if we want to.
Play Battleships
　　if we want to.
Model with plasticine
　　if we want to.
Play chess
　　if we want to.
Connect Four
　　if we want to.
Build with Lego
　　if we want to.
Read comics
　　if we want to.
Use the computer
　　if we want to.
Do Dot-to-Dots
　　if we want to.
Do lots and lots
　　if we want to.

But we can't dash outside
    if we want to.
Splash around
in the puddle-rich
playground
    if we want to.
Run around with mouths open
wide catching raindrops
    if we want to.
Hop, skip, jump
and get soaking wet
    if we want to

Or simply stand
if we want to
and watch a rainbow
start to curve
across the sky
which has been darker
than a school pencil lead
all morning.

Tony Langham

Sir's a Secret Agent

Sir's a secret agent
He's licensed to thrill
At Double-Oh Sevening
He's got bags of skill.

He's tall, dark and handsome
With a muscular frame
Teaching's his profession
But Danger's his game!

He's cool and he's calm
When he makes a decision
He's a pilot, sky-diver
And can teach long-division.

No mission's too big
No mission's too small
School-kids, mad scientists
He takes care of them all.

He sorts out the villains
The spies and the crooks
Then comes back to school
And marks all our books!

Tony Langham

A poem for Scowly-face dragging his feet on the way to school

The rain isn't pouring
The wind isn't blowing
The clouds aren't lowering
Traffic isn't roaring

Why are you?

The streets fresh and gleaming
The air is sparkling
Dogs running joyful
Birds singing, sun smiling

Why aren't you?

Jenny Joseph

Geography Lesson

Our teacher told us one day he would leave
And sail across a warm blue sea
To places he had only known from maps,
And all his life had longed to be.

The house he lived in was narrow and grey
But in his mind's eye he could see
Sweet-scented jasmine clinging to the walls,
And green leaves burning on an orange tree.

He spoke of the lands he longed to visit,
Where it was never drab or cold.
I couldn't understand why he never left,
And shook off the school's stranglehold.

Then halfway through his final term
He took ill and never returned.
He never got to that place on the map
Where the green leaves of the orange trees burned.

The maps were redrawn on the classroom wall;
His name forgotten, he faded away.
But a lesson he never knew he taught
Is with me to this day.

I travel to where the green leaves burn,
To where the ocean's glass-clear and blue,
To places our teacher taught me to love –
And which he never knew.

Brian Patten

Who's Here?

Abby Carter,
Mr Brooks,
Caroline Pycroft
who's just dropped her books;
Darryl Bailey,
Emily Drew,
Fatima Hamon,
Griffith Pugh,
Harry Hancock,
Isobel Poole,
Mr James
who looks after the school;
Karen Parker,
Laura Skinner,
Mrs Murphy

who cooks us our dinner;
Nadim Khan,
Olivia Sweet,
Peter
and Quentin, the brother of Pete;
little Miss Roberts,
Sammy Drew,
Thomas and Tammy,
Uri, who's new.
Then there's Viktor,
William Dack,
Xenia
and Yasmin,
and finally Zak.

Jill Townsend

8

Map

It's a maths lesson but I'm doing geography.
I know this desktop like the back of my hand.
There's a sharp groove chipped in the edge, a valley;
here a small crater gouged near the centre,
inked in, like these names of those who sat

here before me: inked in too deep to be scrubbed out,
as permanent as landscape, coloured like fields or lakes,
marks that only time or deep re-working will erase.
And I have discovered something else:
these scratches on the desktop, these thin paths
that I deepen with the point of my compasses,
have begun to reveal the secret country of my name.

Dave Calder

There was a young lady . . .

There was a young lady of Poole
Who thought she would set up a school;
But all she could teach
Was nine parts of speech
And how to make gooseberry fool.

Anon.

I Am Rubber

I am rubber
You are glue
All the nasty things you say
Rub off me
And stick to you.

Anon.

After the Fire

the new boys' pockets

(ripped from their unpacked shorts
by the blast)

took flight up the stairwell

and settled about the school grounds

like handkerchiefs

        small parachutes

white petals in the grass.

Paul Henry

The Colour of My Dreams

I am a really rotten reader
the worst in all the class
the sort of rotten reader
that makes you want to laugh.

I'm last in all the readin' tests
my score's not on the page
and when I read to teacher
she gets in such a rage.

She says I cannot form my words
she says I can't build up
and that I don't know phonics
– and don't know c-a-t from k-u-p.

They say that I'm dyslexic
(that's a word they've just found out)
. . . but when I get some plasticine
I know what that's about.

I make these scary monsters
I draw these secret lands
and get my hair all sticky
and paint on all me hands.

I make these super models
I build these smashing towers
that reach up to the ceiling
and take me hours and hours.

I paint these lovely pictures
in thick green drippy paint
that gets all on the carpet
and makes the cleaners faint.

I build great magic forests
weave bushes out of string
and paint pink panderellos
and birds that really sing.

I play my world of real believe
I play it every day
and people stand and watch me
but don't know what to say.

They give me diagnostic tests
they try out reading schemes
but none of them will ever know
the colour of my dreams.

Peter Dixon

Four O'clock Friday

Four o'clock Friday, I'm home at last.
Time to forget the week that's past.
On Monday, in break they stole my ball
And threw it over the playground wall.
On Tuesday afternoon, in games
They threw mud at me and called me names.
On Wednesday, they trampled my books on the floor,
So Miss kept me in because I swore.
On Thursday, they laughed after the test
'Cause my marks were lower than the rest.
Four o'clock Friday, at last I'm free,
For two whole days they can't get at me.

John Foster

The Inspectors' Report

Strengths of the school
The tiles in the entrance hall are very shiny
all the footballs in the PE store were full of air
on Tuesday we saw a dinner lady smile.
The white lines on the yard are straight
except when they are supposed to be curvy
the paints in the cupboards are very colourful
and the glue in the glue pots is very sticky.

Weaknesses of the school
Year Three, Year Four, Year Five and Year Six
know very little
English, science or mathematics
also they appear to be
entirely ignorant of music,
geography, history, technology,
PE, RE and ICT
though the little so and so's
achieve very high standards
in tricks with yo-yos.

Year Six
These really are
the worst class we have ever seen!
We mean EVER.
In the entire WORLD.
Their teacher agrees
he's just resigned!

Key points for action
Once we have found where
the head teacher is hiding
we'll let him know.

David Harmer

The Great Shove Ha'penny Craze

When I was a boy
there was one game
we played endlessly at school.

Shove ha'penny.
(That's short for half penny.)
Of course, we don't have those now.

But you can still play the game
with a couple of two pence pieces
and a five pence bit.

You need a long table
with a smooth, shiny surface,
and a six inch ruler.

Then you play football. Really.
You take it in turns to shove your two pences
and knock the ball (the 5p) around.

You aim for his goal.
He aims for yours.
Just like the real thing.

Sometimes you have to defend,
shove your 'man' behind the ball
or knock it (the 5p) out of play.

If you're smart you can play
with four two pences.
That takes skill, that does.

Try it. It's addictive.
It will only cost you nine pence
and it won't give you eye strain.

Tip: just don't tell your dad.
Unless you want ear ache –
or a challenge.

Chris d'Lacey

The School Goalie's Reasons Why Each Goal Shouldn't Have Been a Goal in a Match That Ended 14:0 to the Visiting Team

1. It wasn't fair, I wasn't ready . . .
2. Their striker was offside, it was obvious . . .
3. Phil got in my way, he always gets in my way, he should be dropped . . .
4. I had something in my eye . . .
5. I hadn't recovered from the last one that went in, or the one before that . . .
6. I thought I heard our head teacher calling my name . . .
7. Somebody exploded a blown-up crisp bag behind me . . .

8. There was a beetle on the pitch, I didn't want to tread on it . . .

9. Somebody exploded another blown-up crisp bag . . .

10. That girl in Year 5 was smiling at me, I don't like her doing that . . .

11. The goalposts must have been shifted, they weren't as wide before . . .

12. I thought I saw a UFO fly over the school . . .

13. There was a dead ringer for David Beckham watching us, he was spooky . . .

And goal number 14?

It just wasn't a goal, I'm sorry, it just wasn't a goal and that's that.

OK?

Brian Moses

Awe and Wonder

Today we did 'awe and wonder' worksheets
with Mrs Holmcroft and the helper lady
whose name I do not know.
Mrs Holmcroft showed us a beautiful daffodil
and the school pond . . .
but Darren didn't see the pond
because he gets asthma
and had to stay behind with the lady
whose name I do not know.
Afterwards we went into the hall
to listen to beautiful music,
then Mrs Holmcroft read us a beautiful poem
in a voice we had never heard before –
but Darren got sent out for laughing.
After dinner we did some awe and wonder painting.
Mrs Holmcroft said we could do a daffodil,
with tones and hues,
or a beautiful pattern,
but not the pond.
Darren did bombs and aeroplanes
because he thought Mrs Holmcroft had said war and
    thunder.

Peter Dixon

Poem about the Injustice of Being Made to Stand Outside in the Rain at Break-time

I't's
Not
Fair

Sue Hardy-Dawson

B is for Books

They told me that reading
Was a magical gift,
A glassy key to unlock secret doors
That hid amongst the rustling paper walls.

And if I could only crack the spidery code
That crawled before my confused eyes,
They said I would discover
A treasure chest of wonders:
Tiny beasts with jewelled tusks;
Talking mirrors; enchanted swords;
Singing green stones.

They promised me forests and friendly wolves;
Dragons and diamond mines;
Sleepy palaces and spiral staircases –
But all they ever gave me
Was another book,
Harder and more unreadable
Than the one before.

Clare Bevan

Trouble Ahead

The teacher took a head count.
I fooled her by taking mine off,
And hiding it in my desk.

At dinnertime, still feeling headstrong,
I pushed to the head of the queue.
Keen to make headlines in the school magazine,
I headed a bread pudding across the canteen.

Then the Head caught me.

Simon Pitt

Spring Assembly

Right! As you all know,
It's spring pretty soon
And I want a real good one this year.
I want no slackers. I want SPRING!
That's S-P-R-I-N-G! Got it?
Spring! Jump! Leap!
Energy! Busting out all over!
Nothing so beautiful! Ding-a-ding-a-ding!

Flowers: I want a grand show from you –
Lots of colour, lots of loveliness.
Daffodils: blow those gold trumpets.
Crocuses: poke up all over the parks and gardens,
Yellows, purples, whites; paint that picture.
And a nice show of blossom on the fruit trees.
Make it look like snow, just for a laugh,
Or loads of pink candy floss.

Winds: blow things about a bit.
North, South, East, West, get it all stirred up.
Get March nice and airy and exciting.

Rain: lots of shimmering showers please.
Soak the earth after its winter rest.
Water those seeds and seedlings.
And seeds: Start pushing up.
Up! Up! Up! Let's see plenty of green.

Sunshine! Give the earth a sparkle
After the rain. Warm things up.

And you birds: I haven't forgotten you.
Fill the gardens with song.
Build your nests (you'll remember how).
And you lambs: set an example,
Jump, leap, bound, bounce, spring!

And kids: ditch those coats and scarves,
And get running and skipping.
Use that playground, none of this
Hanging about by the school wall
With your hands in your jeans pockets.
It's spring, I tell you.
And you're part of it
And we've got to have a real good one this year.

Gerard Benson

Tank

In the beginning, the Tank was void –
all dust and sealant, thumbprints on glass.
And Miss Greene looked down upon the emptiness and
  said,
Let there be gravel, to the depth of one inch.
And lo, there was gravel – boil-washed, sifted,
steeped at an incline from front wall to back.

Then said Miss Greene, *Let there be stone rising out of
this gravel that shall gnarl and bend and make arches
in the void*. And from out of the pebbles there came
forth a bridge, and the keep of a castle, and a sunken
chest. And around these things the children placed
pondweed and all other forms of oxygenating plant.

So it came to pass that water filled the void
and the pondweed did flourish and the stones drew
colour from within themselves. And on the third day,
when all was ready with the Tank, Miss Greene held
the children by their hands and said, *Our work is done.
Let there be fish*.

And into the Tank came Buzz and Fizz and Jazz the
    Shubunkins,
Tizz the Oranda, Walter the Weatherloach.
And Miss Greene scattered flakes upon the surface of the
water and the fish did eat and were exceeding happy.
And even as the school bell rang that night and darkness
    came
to lie upon the Tank, Miss Greene put aside her marking
and said, *Let there be light*. And a neon light shone.

And the children and Miss Greene were happy in this,
and fed the fish and took pleasure in their swimming.

This is how the world called 'RECEPTION' was created.

And the Head, upon seeing this, knew that it was good.

Chris d'Lacey

Boy at the Somme

'The last one there is a cow pat!'
grinned the small boy
running between the white headstones
as he began the one hundred metre dash
along the narrow strip of turf separating
Private Tom Atkins, age 18, of the Lancashire Fusiliers,
from Lieutenant Edward Hollis, age 19,
of the Seaforth Highlanders;
more than twice the distance they managed
over the same small field
that October morning eighty-seven years before
into the spitting venom of the machine guns
that killed them instantly.

Alan Durant

Windy Playground

They played blow-me-down in the yard,
letting the wind bully them,
coats above heads, arms spread wide,
daring the wind to do its worst.
They leant forward against the blow
as it rallied and flung them back,
then coats puffed out like clouds
they returned to attack the blast,
while the gale drew a breath and then
pressed relentless. Till wild in defeat
and magnificent, they grouped again
and stretched their wings, stubborn
as early airmen.

Brian Moses

The Owl Man's Visit

The Owl Man comes in.
He stops and stares,
His eyes unblinking and brown.
He swoops to a cage,
Whirls off the black cloth
And that's when he wheels around.

Now on his gloved hand
A Snowy Owl flaps
Flashing frost as he fans out his wings.
The Owl Man twitters
And hums in his throat
As the great bird flutters and clings.

The Snowy Owl stills
To his master's tune,
Then preens his snow feathers and blinks
And his eyes are black ice
Like the Owl Man's eyes
And between them a strange, close link.

And whenever at night
An owl keens,
Woo, Woo, his wintry song,
I think of the two –
Man and bird – at the school
And their wild, wordless bond.

Mal Lewis Jones

The Trees Behind the Teachers' Cars
Spring Term

Emerald tips are
twinkling in the light,
drinking down the light,
thinking of opening up and soaking up the light
this afternoon,
or sometime soon.
That'll be a treat for Sir's car.

Kate Williams

Elvin

For twenty-one days we'd turned the eggs –
now noughts, now crosses,
(that's how we'd marked them)
and filled in the chart.

The infants came into our class
to see the incubator and learn
about hatching and stuff.
We promised to let them know.

Today, day twenty-two, Alan saw the crack.
We all took turns watching.
Jill and Jacqueline stayed in all playtime.
The crack got bigger.

While we were eating dinner, ravioli again,
and apple crumble with pink custard,
Elvin hatched out.
He was fluffy brown, not fluffy yellow.

We all stroked him.
It was lucky we called him, 'him',
because later we found out
he would grow up to be a cockerel.

But actually we called him Elvin
because of Mrs Elvin, our caretaker,
who's great and doesn't mind mess at all.
Just as well, with all that straw and sawdust.

Catherine Benson

Sticking the Stars

I coloured in a toucan
I did two tigers too
I made a card for mummy
and another one for you.
 I printed
 and I patterned
 stuck pasta on a plate
 wrote my name in pencil
 did numbers 1 to 8.
Then I did a bit of writing
but writing is too hard
so I thought of mud and digging

instead of Easter cards . . .
I dreamed of being a four wheel
in a playground park for cars
making camps
          and puddles
instead of sticking stars.

Peter Dixon

Easter in School

We've practised all the Easter hymns
And brought in eggs to boil.
We've made them into 'egg heads'
(Mine's a Martian dressed in foil)

We've all made tissue daffodils
To take home to our mums,
Baked Easter Bunny biscuits
(And licked up all the crumbs!)

It's Friday, end-of-term at last!
We're busy making cards.
We're using best art paper
And I'm sharing mine with Harj.

I've pasted on bright flowers, a chick,
A golden sun above,
A glitter Happy Easter
And inside **With lots of love.**

I sneak a look at Harj's card.
'Hey, Harj, what's that big splosh?'
'That's the green hill far away,' she says.
'And that's the cross.'

Patricia Leighton

Pencil

I want to write
but the pencil fights
my fingers:
it judders
it slides
so that out becomes but
and now turns to how
and my a tangles itself
into an interesting knot –
it's too strong, this pencil,
however hard I try

it slips to one side
and makes pot into got
or dab into bad
and if I try m or w
it just wants to wobble on
till it's drawn the sea.

I know what's wrong
I've been given
a doodling pencil
that likes to scribble
and make a mess.

What I need is a pencil
that wants to write

Dave Calder

End of Term Reports

Pinocchio's been lying again.
He's such a naughty boy.
He will not do his work
and seems determined to annoy.

Snow White's been good as usual
the Home Economics prize
goes to her for the second time
for excellent apple pies.

Sleeping Beauty's had a bad term –
she can't stay asleep at all.
Cinderella's fallen out with her
for wanting to go to the ball.

Jack's failed Biology again –
his beanstalk fails to flourish.
He's developed a fear of giants.
He must work on his courage.

Parents' evenings will be held
a week next Tuesday night.
Please return the tear-off slip
Yours, Mrs Everight.

Angela Topping

April

April 1st

Our teacher's looking nervous,
I think she's feeling tense –
sixty eyes all watch her closely,
we're tingling with suspense.

She shrewdly tests her chair seat,
before daring to sit down –
her eyes flick, spy like, round the room
under a worried frown.

She peers into her pencil pot
as if it's going to bite –
and slowly takes her pencil out
to check before she writes.

Our thirty watchful faces
all tell that something's up –
then her attention fastens
on her waiting coffee cup.

'I think I'll leave my coffee,
till after registration,
I apologize if this frustrates
your keen anticipation!'

She opens up the register,
says, 'It's very quiet in school . . .'
then out it jumps, and she screams AAAARGH!
and we scream, 'APRIL FOOL!'

Liz Brownlee

The Last Boy to School

The last boy to school
counts drifting sheep
between the dreaming clouds.

The last boy to school
follows snails' silver trails
down the slow winding path.

The last boy to school
feels each shade of green
that gleams in the glistening trees.

The last boy to school
sees no need
for the rulers,
the set squares, the text books:

his head is filled
with the whole of the world.

Dave Ward

Late

His eyes watch as the seconds tick
Past the appointed hour.
He sniggers at detention
While he marvels at his power.
'Perhaps I'll give him lines today,
That's something that he'll hate.'
A frantic run outside the door
An evil smile
'You're late.'

Violet Macdonald

The School Nature Table

Here's our collection,
it's all on display.
This feather, for instance,
fell from a jay.
Here's some glossy brown conkers,
an acorn or two,
an eggshell of delicate,
powdery blue,
an owl pellet, knobbly
with tiny white bones
and, from a pine tree,
some giant, scaly cones.
Here's a dinosaur's tooth,
an adder's shed skin,
some sycamore seeds
with a whirligig spin,
a mummified frog,
some poppy seed heads,
a skeleton leaf,
a jar of bright red

papery poppies,
petals all dropping,
some brown, dried-up seaweed,
the sort you like popping
and this piece of amber,
like a small jewel
on our nature table,
the best in the school.

Marian Swinger

Rules of the Game

Our school has no field so we can only play
football in the yard – and it's small, so Thursday
is when we're allowed to bring in our balls –
and that's the first rule. I've noticed that all
games need rules, and in each game there are some
you can't play without – like if you throw one
when you play snakes and ladders, that's how far
you must move, but you could agree to start
at the top and go down ladders and up the snakes
and still have a good game. So it doesn't make
much difference to us if there's five on one
side and six on the other, or if we all run

113

together after the ball and don't have a goalie –
you understand – rules are just what you agree
among yourselves – over the wire fence is definitely
off the pitch and getting in the big boys' way
is asking for trouble. Being rude to the janitor
will get you sent inside and kicking spectators
or their lunch-boxes is not allowed –
you have to tolerate the crowd
and you might start a fight that stops the game.
Most of the simple rules we keep the same,
no hands or fists, no deliberate tripping,
no pulling shirts until they tear, no sitting
on the ball unless you're really in goal.
That's about it. But playing after the bell's gone
could mean suspension. And you'd be a total nit-wit
to pick up the ball and run away with it.
That's not playing the same game any more.
That's rugby, or a declaration of war.

Dave Calder

I Love to Do My Homework

I love to do my homework,
It makes me feel so good.
I love to do exactly
As my teacher says I should.

I love to do my homework,
I never miss a day.
I even love the men in white
Who are taking me away.

Anon.

If Only . . .

If only I could catch the stars
And trap them in a Kilner jar
Like silvery bright atoms.

If only I could steal a comet's tail
And tie it to a ship's sail
So that it could illuminate the sea
When the days get too dark.

If only I could snatch
A clown's mask and place it
On the twisted face of sadness.

If only I could freeze the sun
And hand out slices of frozen light
Like leaflets on a street corner
Or a deck of cold calling cards.

If only I could imprison electricity's
dazzling spark like a vein of lightning
And use it to tingle your toes.

If only I could poke a hole
Into every spiteful jibe,
As barbed as a nettle's bite.

If only I could take you home
Wrapped in an anorak of words.

I could use you in my next poem –
You'd make an explosive opening!

Pie Corbett

School Clubs

Miss Weaver does the Maypole club
– dancing in and out.
Ms Bongo does the drumming
– helped by Mr Grout.
Miss Slurry does the pottery
Count Basie takes the band
Miss Emins does the sculpture
     with tents and bags of sand.
We love handball and gardens
ballet is just great
cooking is terrific and no one's ever late . . .

You'll have to sign up swiftly
clubs are always fun
they fill up very quickly
except – that is –

SIGN UP HERE
FOR APOSTROPHE
**, ' , ** CLUB

**, , **

ARE
FUN.

just one!

Peter Dixon

Green School

The school has gone green,
an allotment's being made
and we're wearing wellies
and carrying spades.
We're digging the ground up,
we're planting the seeds,
we're making a compost heap
out of the weeds.
We'll be growing tomatoes
and three kinds of bean,

118

potatoes and pumpkins,
the biggest you've seen
and cabbages, carrots,
cucumbers and peas
and a few marigolds
for attracting the bees.
We're the new eco army,
all of us keen
on changing the world
now the school has gone green.

Marian Swinger

Fraction

Three's no good
Because three is always two and one
And I am never in the two.

You are in the two –
In every two there's ever been
There's something in you that the others want.

I can see it,
Even though it doesn't have a name
It's a sort of *shine* that I might share beside a two

But I'm the third one
In the three.

Jan Dean

In the School Garden

In the willow's bend
is the forest's fuse

in the orchard tree
is the tang of juice

in the flowerbed
is the earthworm's work

in the chains of the trail
is the iron from the rock

in the blue bench
is the pinewood's smell

in the gaps in the seat
is the wind's finger

in the bark by the path
is the woodland rain

in the weather vane
is the gull's wing beat

in the willow tunnel
is the child's delight

in the night-time garden
is the snuff and scuffle

of a class of creatures
creeping to study

the wind's voice
under the moon's cool eye.

Maggie Norton

Amazing Maisie
for Julia Densham

Almost crystal clear,
honest,
as if inside her *see-through* skin,
Maisie was made of liquid glass;

could stand at the front
of our class,
yet not get in the way.

OK, maybe
some reflections and refraction
and no one could forget fantastic
prism shimmers,
as her body split white light
into glimmering bands of
red, orange, yellow, green, blue . . .

Truly amazing:
on lazy days of blazing sun,
strange rainbows played
over everyone.

Mike Johnson

Lunchtime Swaps

Roll up, roll up for lunchtime swaps,
Take out your boxes and flip off the tops.
Two cheese sarnies for one of ham?
Peanut butter for strawberry jam?

Mini-Cheddars, crunchy and tasty,
For Tandoori chicken, yummy and spicy?
Salad bap? Do you think I'm dumb?
Yeh, I know, but try telling my mum.

A savoury dip with crusty bread sticks
For a Caribbean fruit and nut mix?
One iced cake for a sherbet bomb?
Seems fair to me. OK, you're on.

Fruity yoghurts and slurpy smoothies
All have us absolutely drooling.
Chocolates and sweets are sure-fire swaps
And if you've got crisps it's top-of-the-pops.

Apples and oranges, cherries and plums,
Melon slices and mango chunks,
No matter what mum packs, it's always true
Someone's got something better than you!

Patricia Leighton

There once was a teacher from Leeds

There once was a teacher from Leeds,
Who swallowed a packet of seeds.
In less than an hour,
Her nose was a flower,
And her hair was a bunch of weeds.

Anon.

The Happy Memories Bench
*(for pupils, past and present, of
Colwall Primary School, Malvern)*

There's a school that I know
at the foot of a wide, green hill.
There's a bench that I know
and old tractor tyres
tumbling with jumbles of flowers.

A football field
creamy with clover
and over the way
a playground with tracks
for blue shoes, a snail maze,
stepping stones.

In the school that I know
there's a painted grey castle
to run through,
a log fort and bridge,
a wood shelter with seats,
picnic tables, a pond.

And in summer the outside
is wide and alive
with races and chases,
hopping and skipping,
shouts, squeals and laughter
that echo below
the green hill that I know.

There's a plate made of brass
on the bench that I know.

Happy Memories
David, Richard, Andrew, Joanna

it says.

I know.
I know.

Patricia Leighton

Dragonships

They set sail (huge sails!)
for our land of grain,
raided the coast,
pierced our fields,
our villages,
by river

slicing through water in longships,
slipping
silent as eels . . .

each ship powered
by a score and a half of oarsmen
terrible men in terrible ships . . .

sometimes a dragonship,
like the dragons that lurk
in our rivers,
envenoming our waters,
bringing death
as surely as the monsters from the north.

Joan Poulson

*The phrase 'envenom our waters' is adapted from a C7th
manuscript. For centuries, it was common belief that dragons of
all sizes lived in British rivers, streams and lakes. The danger was
in the disease they carried.*

The Estuary Field Trip

I walked with my class along the estuary
The salty wind sneaked through the cracked concrete
of time-worn sea defences,
stirred the weeds and rusty wire
that criss-crossed the caked mud bed

Children poked under rocks
hunting for crabs
and tugged at a limp of driftwood,
perhaps once part of a sailing barge
taking bricks to London

Isn't it beautiful, I said
Richard looked up at me, nodded, smiled
A rare moment
A mystical union of teacher and pupil
Mr Stevens, he said,
Did you see the Man U game last night?

Roger Stevens

Up in Smoke

Cornelius loved Chemistry
It had a strange attraction
The final words he spoke were 'Sir?
'Is this a chain reaction?'

Paul Bright

If You Were a Carrot

If you were a carrot
and I was a sprout
I'd boil along with you
I'd sit on your plate

If you were a tadpole
and I was a frog
I'd wait till your legs grew
I'd teach you to croak

If you were a conker
and I was a string
we'd win every battle
we'd beat everything

If you were a jotter
and I was a pen
I'd write you a message
again and again

If you were a farmer
I'd be in your herd
If you were a popsong
I'd sing every word

I wish I could tell you
that I like you a lot
but you're like a secret
and I'm like a knot.

Berlie Doherty

Girls and Boys Come Out to Play

It's 1954. I'm small.
Girls do handstands against a wall
while boys have gangs which fight and spit.
You're in. You're on. You're out. You're it.

Young cowboys charge and drag their shoes.
They click their tongues to sound like hooves.
Their fingers point to fire a gun.
You're in. You're out. You're it. You're on.

The nurses stroke and feed their dolls.
Footballers score in net-less goals.
A conker splits; you lose or win.
You're on. You're out. You're it. You're in.

It's 1954. I'm small.
Girls in circles sneeze and fall.
A whistle blows. I hear a shout.
You're it. You're in. You're on. You're out.

Steve Turner

School Trip Trauma
(Haiku)

At the museum
we lost Liam. He was in
the queue for the loo.

Kate Williams

Four O'clock Snack

Sandwich
No butter please
Crusty bread, thick cut, some cheese
Lettuce tomato mustard please
Great Stuff!

Angela Topping

Drawing Dragons

On St George's Day, we all drew a dragon.
Rosie's was a love dragon, pink and puffy
with heart-shaped scales and a tail that could
curl round and cuddle you – whole!

Henry's sea dragon lived underwater. It was squirmy,
like a snake, and its fins could turn into wings out of
    water.
It had shells for teeth and claws made of fish bones.
It ate seaweed and jellyfish, but only at night.

A dragon called Greenbig fed on grass.
Mary made him up because her dad was annoyed
that his lawnmower had broken. Greenbig could draw
the white lines on football pitches with his tail.
Sometimes he got hayfever. That made him snuffle.

Amrit drew a dragon called Garbage. It chomped
the rubbish. Baked bean cans were its favourite trash.
Its tummy was a furnace where it burned everything.
When it lifted its tail, it stank! Garbage was a danger,
like global warming.

And me, I had a rainbow dragon. All the colours of
the world were in his scales. He made sick people better
and blew away nightmares with his fire. He wasn't
the type to scare anyone, my dragon. Not even maidens.
He was a saint. So I called him . . . George.

Chris d'Lacey

Poor old teacher

Poor old teacher, we missed you so,
When in hospital you had to go.
For you to remain there is a sin,
We're sorry about the banana skin.

Anon.

Size-Wise

Our teacher Mr Little's really tall.
He's twice the size of our helper Mrs Small.
'Were you big when you were little?'
Sandra asked him.
'I was Little when I was little,
but I've always been big!'
he said with a grin.
'Have you always been small?'
Sandra asked Mrs Small.
'No,' said Mrs Small.
'I was Short before I got married,
then I became Small.
But,' she added, 'I've always been little.'
'That's the long and the short of it,'
said Mr Little.
'I've always been big and Little,
but she used to be little and Short,
and now she's little and Small.'

John Foster

The Weird Dinner Ladies

Scene: Scotland
A desolate place – the playground

Rain pours down. The school bell tolls.

1st Dinner lady:	When shall we three meet again?
	In hailstorm, blizzard or in rain?
2nd Dinner lady:	When there is some peace at last.
	When the morning break has passed.
3rd Dinner lady:	Ten it is then, round half-past.
1st Dinner lady:	And the scene?
2nd Dinner lady:	The old canteen.
3rd Dinner lady:	There to make our fish supreme.
1st Dinner lady:	I'm coming grey Morag
2nd Dinner lady:	Tea break calls.
3rd Dinner lady:	At last!
All:	School dinner's foul and that's not fair,
	Steam of cabbage fogs and fills the air.

Karen Costello-McFeat

A Trip to the Art Gallery

I like this painting the best
because it makes me go Hmm.

It is of a pretty lady
lying down.

Some of the other paintings
make me go Hmm as well
because that is what Miss Heron does
so I do too.

Hmm.

I like the painting of the sunset
that is all red and colours
and also the ones of people in hell
and in heaven
and the one with the dancers.

I went Hmm to those as well
but this one makes me go Hmm the best,
because the lady that the painting is of
looks like she is going Hmm too.

She is lying down
and she is leaning her head
on her hand like this.

Hmm, goes the lady in the painting
and Hmm, I go back to her.

Miss Heron just told me
to stop going Hmm all the time
which isn't fair
because it was her who started it.

So now I am going Hmm
to the lady in the painting
as quietly as the lady in the painting
is going Hmm to me.

Hmm,
we go to each other
as quiet as two paintings in secret.
Hmm.

David Bateman

Waiting

The clock is
Tick   ing
Tantalizingly slowly.
And I'm waiting
Waiting to go in.
Stan's in there now
I can hear him talking
He's probably strapped to an
Elec
Electro
Electrocarda.
A lie detector.

The clock is
Tick   ing
And I'm
Shrink   ing
Into my chair
My heart is pounding
In my chest
And I feel like I'm home
To ten million butterflies.

The clock is
Tick   ing
And I'm watching the door
And I can see him
Walking around inside
Pacing
Back and forth
Forth and back.

The clock is
Tick   ing
And I can see the sun outside
And I fear
This may be the last
I see of it
As the door's opened,
And I've been called
Into the principal's office.

Violet Macdonald

After School

I've saved time for you,
taken a handful of hours and put them in my diary,
folded them tidily between the pages.

It's the perfect gift for someone who's so busy.

You could take me out for tea
or spend twenty minutes on the phone
instead of two. Maybe,
we'll go for a long walk, slowly,
noticing the wrens in the hedges,
stop to watch the high-tailed horses trot in a field.
Perhaps we'll stand still and see the flick
of a mouse under leaves,
if I've saved enough time,
we'll see.

Judith Green

Sum Haiku

All my sums are wrong
I wish I could go home now
Raindrops wash my face

Coral Rumble

May

Experiment

at school we're doing growing things
  with cress.
sprinkly seeds in plastic pots
  of cotton wool.

Kate's cress sits up on the sill
  she gives it water.
mine is shut inside the cupboard
  dark and dry.

now her pot has great big clumps
  of green
mine hasn't.
Mrs Martin calls it Science
  I call it mean.

Danielle Sensier

Happy Birthday St Michaels

Would you believe this year the head said in assembly
our school is one hundred and ten years old
and as a bit of a joke we sang
Happy Birthday to you St Michaels.
Someone's granddad came in last week
who'd been to our school fifty years ago
and he said how different it was then because
everyone sat in proper desks with lids and cold
steel legs and had hard wooden seats fixed to them
and they wrote by dipping a pen with a nib into an inkwell
which was like a little cup with ink in it and
it meant you could flick ink pellets at each other.
The teachers would cane or slipper you
if you were naughty which could just mean talking
and the boys and girls played in different playgrounds
to stop them playing together. Of course
there were no computers or televisions or videos
in his day he said and teachers just wrote
everything up on a blackboard with chalk
and then rubbed it all off when they had finished
with a blackboard rubber with a really hard wooden
    handle
which could also be thrown at naughty children.

He said how it looks more interesting and
much more fun now and it was harder then but
he said he had liked it at our school
and they were the happiest days of his life.
I suppose there won't be anybody left
who went to our school when it was new
and could tell us how it was
they'd have to be about one hundred and fifteen years old.
Funny to think that all those little children
who would have run around then just like us
but in old-fashioned clothes would have grown up
and got old and died and maybe they were the happiest
   days of
their lives too?
I wonder if I'll come back when I'm a granddad
to our school when it's one hundred and sixty years old
and tell everybody what it was like then
which is now
and I wonder if these will have been
the happiest days of my life?

Trevor Parsons

Colouring In

And staying inside the lines
Is fine, but . . .
I like it when stuff leaks –
When the blue bird and the blue sky
Are just one blur of blue blue flying,
And the feeling of the feathers in the air
And the wind along the blade of wing
Is a long gash of smudgy colour.
I like it when the flowers and the sunshine
Puddle red and yellow into orange,
The way the hot sun on my back
Lulls me – muddles me – sleepy
In the scented garden,
Makes me part of the picture . . .
Part of the place.

Jan Dean

Catch a Rainbow

If I could catch a rainbow

I'd hang it round your shoulders.
A rainbow scarf.
Its pot of gold
next to the beat of your heart.

If I could catch a rainbow

I'd make
rainbow puddles.
For you to splash colour
wherever your steps may take you.

If I could catch a rainbow

I'd turn it upside down.
A rainbow rocking bed
to let you float to a land of bliss,
drift safe on dozing dreams.

If I could catch a rainbow.

Brian Whittingham

The Soggy End of Science

I'm sitting at the soggy end of science;
Can't grasp how it works, but value each
Electrical appliance.
I try to understand
But my brain is in defiance,
So I'm fumbling at the foggy end of science.

I'm stumbling at the sticky edge of science;
Though fascinating facts intrigue my mind
I'm not up with the intellectual giants,
I try to follow theories
But my brain shows no compliance,
So I'm tripping at the tricky edge of science.

Celia Warren

Rumour

Whisper, whisper.
Something cruel
is being said
around the school.

Wriggle, giggle,
this is fun.
Have you heard
what she has done?

Not such fun
to be left out
'cos you're the one
they talk about.

Jill Townsend

Summer

I can hear grass growing
through this open window.
It doesn't have to know
about multiplication;
it just gets on with it.
I wish it would speed up
and swallow this room;
make it a jungle where
we could hunt for adders
to help with our maths,
or those large snakes
to tell us about
Pythonagoras' theorem.

John C. Desmond

Miss Flotsam

Miss Flotsam was my reception teacher
She had travelled the world
Brown hair turned golden under distant suns
Clothes carrying colours from countless corners of
   continents.

When my mother's face spilled
A gush of adolescent tears
At the school gates
Miss Flotsam soaked up the drops
In Peruvian alpaca
Caught splashes in Himalayan singing bowls
Let sobs fall on Indonesian Gamelans.

Miss Flotsam had flown through air pockets in Jumbo jets
Sailed the seven seas in opposite directions
Cycled through cyclones with dengue fever
Soothed mothers when their hearts cracked.

When Gavin punched me for being too brown
Miss Flotsam glared at him
With an eye that could turn fists into begging bowls.

When my mother was late
Miss Flotsam read to me –
Stories of imperfect families and unexpected heroes.

When I dozed in class
Miss Flotsam let me sleep –
Sleep through math
Sleep through break
Sleep through lunch
Sleep through the home time bell.

When I was naughty Miss Flotsam told me off
Asked if everything was OK at home?
And smiled at my lies.

Miss Flotsam had climbed peaks circled by vultures.
Waded rivers with unseen bottoms
Bought ugly fruits in foreign languages in dusty markets
Helped mothers too ashamed to know something was
    wrong
Helped pupils too young to ask for help.

Miss Flotsam was amazing.

Joseph Coelho

Silent Pee

Today in English
we did silent letters
The 'g' in cough
The 'b' in debtors
Teacher asked each of us
for an example
Brainbox Julian
gave her ample
When at last
she turned to me
I told her clearly
'Silent pee in sea'

Susan Bates

The Photograph

In the picture on our classroom wall –
a framed photograph, black and white,
of a classroom 50 years ago –
it's as if the children are staring out
at our classroom now.
They look happy enough

and seem unaware
of the prison-like bareness of their room,
or the strictly separated rows
and iron hardness of their desks,
or their cheap and coarsely woven clothes,
or the cane hung ready on the wall
or the teacher, suited, with slicked-back hair,
who looks like he would guiltlessly use it.
They seem happy enough

and look, no doubt, beyond the visiting photographer
to the home time bell.
To mums in aprons or pinafores
and dads who, by and large,
smoked pipes and wore flat caps
and twiddled with the wireless set,

while they played chase in terraced streets
and made up the life of their days.
They look happy enough

and seem unaware
they have been caught and thrown aboard
a flimsy craft, sailing for the future,
that's happened to catch the wind.

Trevor Parsons

Lace Trouble

Everyone is ready for PE except me.
Short shorts, armless tops
Trainers;
Nike Trainers
Reebok trainers
Matchstick trainers
Trainers with lights
Trainers with pumps
Trainers with wheels
Trainers with laces!

Horrid, horrible, confusing laces!
Snake-like, worm-like, squiggerly nasty laces.

Everyone is filing into the playground except me
Trainers jumping
Trainers hopping
Trainers skipping.

I don't know how to tie my laces –
Mum has shown me several times
Dad has tried too
But every time I have a go
I can't make the loops do what I want them to.

I make a knot in one
But never both ends
I tangle them up in a heartbeat
I twist and criss-cross
But they come un-done
Or fall off if I cough.

I'm in the classroom
Laces in a pile by my toes
My classmates are playing rounders
It ought to be my go.

Jason is batting
I know I'm better than him
If I could just do up my laces
My side is sure to win.

Mark comes into class
He plays for the other team
He sees me standing in my laces
His smile becomes a beam.

'Lace trouble' he says and I just want to hit him
I'm sure he's laughing inside
If I had my plimsoles on I'd get him.

Mark bends down to my feet
Holds my laces aloft
It's taking all my strength not to tell him to 'just go away'
He explains in detail
How to thread and weave a lace
Not only a single knot but double and triple ties!

Trainers running for rounders balls
Trainers skidding
Trainers sliding in the mud
My trainers are tied tight
Secured to my feet.
And I did it!
I tied them!
I knotted!
I weaved!
I need never worry again
If my laces limp
And I have a new friend
He plays for the other side
Yet every time he scores a goal
I cheer a little inside.

Joseph Coelho

Who Lives in the School Pond?

Water boatmen rowing home
Water spiders skip and scurry
Tiny fish dart through the weeds
Pond skaters in a hurry
Dragonflies with whizzing wings
Their turquoise bodies catch the light
Worms who live down in the mud
Fat old frogs who hide from sight
It's like a complicated play
I'd like to stay and watch all day

Roger Stevens

Mrs Harrison

I was always complimenting her
Playing all her favourite CDs
Helping tidy, handing out forms
And combing out her pet dog's fleas.
I washed her car during playtime
I gave her an apple each day
And made her a card saying 'Thank you'
But she gave me an 'F' anyway.

Celina Macdonald

At Lunchtime

After lunch,
In that half hour or so
Before lessons start again
And if it's fine
I go outside
And sit on the wall.

Some boys like to stand around in groups
And talk,
Others like to play football –
But me? I like just sitting on the wall,
Watching everybody else,
Watching all the world go by,
Just for a while.

Some people think I'm strange,
But I don't mind:
I like to think I'm not the kind
Of person who does things
Other people do
Just because they want him to;

I like to think that I'm OK
Exactly as I am –

That's why I'll stay
Sitting on the wall
Watching all the world go by,
Just for a while . . .

Gillian Floyd

Flying

Every time
The wind is high,
Terry Ashworth
Tries to fly.

He fastens a pole
Across his back,
Makes wings with a pair
Of polythene sacks,

And rushes
Up and down the yard,
Trying hard
To have lift-off.

But although
We all of us
Give him space,
And he travels
At a terrific pace,

He always stays
With his feet
On the ground;
He says it's his boots
That hold him down.

Irene Rawnsley

16

Tadpoles
For J. W.

Since my first infant term I remember
their surprise arrivals brought a pleasure
keen and not predicted by the calendar.

One morning you would see glass glint, feel squirms
of fascination rippling into grins.
Our teachers took down old aquariums

from cupboard tops. We rinsed them clean of dust
then filled them with sieved pond-water at first.
After that for topping up the tap sufficed.

One overflowing year Mike Cotton came
with an enamel bucket brimming spawn –
too much for classroom conservation.

Everybody took a handful
in lunchbox, jar or milkbottle.
My plastic bag leaked a trickle

of sticky seepage that ran down
my legs and prompted curious frowns
on faces on the bus back home.

They hatched and grew fat on the windowsill
safe in a flower-vase untouched until
(come round to help a bit) my Aunty Jill

poured them accidentally down the toilet,
then said the family must have something desperate.
My mother never quite forgave her that.

Philip Tupper fed them one by one
to his piranha. Lizzie kept hers in
a bowl until her puppy drank them. When

Jemma's died she pressed them all like leaves
between the pages of a book. Now these
dippings into childhood pools draw symphonies

into a single jar intense and bright
with remembered water, sky and weed and light:
the crotchets quivering their silent music.

Barrie Wade

Shorthand

Our English teacher's
punctuated.

Our Music teacher's
crotchet.

Our Science teacher's
fractal.

But our Humanities teacher's
tropic.

Joan Poulson

Late Again

Off to school,
I'm late again,
hurrying, scurrying
down the lane
past the oak tree,
past the gate
where the white cat
sits and waits,
past the postman,
past old Mabel
putting bird seed
on a table,
past Mr Bates
who's pruning roses,
past his fat black
spaniel, Moses
to where the crossing

lady stands
lollipop
clutched in her hands.
All the traffic
has to wait.
It toots, it hoots,
'You're late! You're late!'

Marian Swinger

There was a teacher from Niger

There was a teacher from Niger,
Who went for a ride on a tiger.
Not long after that,
The tiger got fat,
With the lady from Niger inside her.

Anon.

French Lessons

Oh, Miss Annette Picard-Dubois!
How I love you from afar!

I wish you were not quite so distant.
You are my favourite teaching assistant.

All of my other teachers are bores.
The only lessons I need are yours.

You are the one *que je adore*.
You always leave me wanting *encore*.

For you, I'll sit on the very front bench.
And I might even try learning French.

David Bateman

A Multiplication of One

Nature started very small, as far we can tell,
beginning in the oceans as tiny single cells
and everything alive today arose from that one source:
whale, giraffe and elephant, crocodile and horse,
spider, shrimp and scorpion, crab, fly, fish and flea
all had their origins in the vast primordial seas.
Frog and salamander, lizard, bird and bat,
kangaroo and human, monkey, badger, cat,
tree, grass, moss and flower, bacteria and mite
are branches of the same tree,
with all the world's delights
intertwined, connected, the tiny and the tall
each depending on the other, the greatest on the small,
all springing from this one world, everything from one,
on this blue-green planet beneath its friendly sun.

Marian Swinger

Forbidden Territory

The bell goes!
Whoosh!
Down the corridor we helter-skelter on imaginary
    toboggans,
Or
Vroom!
Skate along the glassy floor arms spread-eagled
To skim the corner,
And
Stop dead
At the headmaster's room.
Squeak across the hall on tip-toe trainers,
Sidle past the lab,
Where Mr Jones keeps his bones,
Then double quick through the double doors,
To burst into the back yard,
And secret country.
Forbidden territory.

As silent as snakes we slip past the No Entry sign,
Creep through the tall grass and peek round the side of the
   shed.
Snuffling, excited, we stifle our laughter,
Stand stock-still,
And listen to the school-keeper,
In full voice,
Singing to his sunflowers.

Mary Green

Headmistress

Get out of my sight
the teacher said
which was fine with me,
I would rather be out here, on my own
than in there any day.
It's peaceful.
And I don't have to show off.
My legs are tired though, slouched down
with my back against the wall.

In the corridor,
there's nowhere to hide.
And she never made a sound.
Too late, I see her, moving towards me
on unseen feet, Sister Serafina.
Hands hidden in her black bell sleeves, she conserves
    energy.
Sent out of class, again
It's not a question.
Go to my office and wait for me there
I'm in despair.

On her desk, we know, she keeps white tissues,
billowing out of a flowery box.
If she offers me one, I'll cry.
I tuck my hands into my sleeves and wait.

Danielle Sensier

Girl with a Worksheet in a Castle

There's a castle we visit where Mr Barret talks
     battlements, baileys and barbicans.

But when I've done my worksheet and my sketches,
     down unsafe stairs I find this lonely place,

this earth-floored larder. I breathe deeply in
     the stink of centuries. An ancient chef

sweats. Humps sacks of onions, spuds,
     turnips and garlic. Thinks of wine and oil

he'll baste over mutton, pork or fish. I hear
     salt Saxon shouts. Alone, I'm history

and history is me. But still . . . be still . . .
                        Then

    Mr Barret's calling *Eleanor Smith*!

He asks me about battlements and baileys,
     and, not this lonely place, this worksheet.

Fred Sedgwick

Thirteen Questions You Should Be Prepared to Answer if You Lose Your Ears at School

Are they clearly named?
When did you notice they were missing?
Were they fixed on properly?
What colour are they?
What size?
Have you looked in the playground?
Did you take them off for PE?
Could somebody else have picked them up by mistake?
Have you felt behind the radiators?
Did you lend them to anybody?
Have you searched the bottom of your bag?
Does the person you sit next to have a similar pair?
Are you sure you brought them to school this morning?

John Coldwell

Not a Nightingale

Today my teacher said I mustn't sing
Because I had a voice like a crab.
Or did he say a frog?
I don't know which, but
Crab or frog, it's all the same.
He didn't say a nightingale.
So after school I took a walk
Along the lane, to where
The cows live in the field.
And I climbed on the gate
And I threw back my head
And I opened my mouth
And I SANG.

And those cows – they stood in a row
And looked at me, and listened,
And then they nodded their great heads,
Up and down, very slow, very gentle,
Just like Grandma's at the school concert.

My teacher says I sound like a crab.
Or a frog? I don't know which.
But those cows don't care.
They *like* the noise I make.
And so do I.

                              Jennifer Curry

Silent Song

I find
A small, white egg
Under the conker tree
In the corner of the school field

I hold
The small, white egg
In the palm of my hand
And look up into the tangled branches

The tree
Is empty and the
Small, white egg
Is cold

I think
There is a song inside
The small, white egg
That we will never hear

Roger Stevens

A Teacher's Epitaph

Here lies a teacher named Ivan Infection,
Who screamed if our work was in need of correction,
Who shouted all day and demanded perfection,
Whose voice was so loud we wore ear-drum protection . . .
He's silent at last, for his Final Inspection.

Clare Bevan

Good Girls

Good girls
will always go like clockwork
home from school,

through the iron gates
where clambering boys
whisper and pull,

past houses
where curtains twitch
and a fingery witch beckons,

by the graveyard
where stone angels stir,
itching their wings,

past tunnelled woods
where forgotten wolves wait
for prey,

past dens
and caves and darknesses
they go like clockwork;

and when they come
to school again
their homework's done.

Irene Rawnsley

30

Bladderwrack

Last half-term we had a trip to the seaside.
Smell of salt, wind in our ears,
Our faces tingle as we descend the cliff.
Small rocks and pebbles chase us to the beach.
We stand on the wall and peer at the horizon.

The tide goes out, stones gleam in the sun.
Grains of sand wash in tiny waves.
Small pools form as the sand dips and crinkles.
Off with shoes, we walk warily over the stones.

Fish net in hand we forage in the pools.
Little crabs, worms, cockles, molluscs
Struggle under the water, which soon evaporates.
We put specimens in our buckets, turn for the shore.

Breakwaters stretch their fingers to the estuary.
Covered in seaweed, which foretells the weather –
We pop the brown hard sprigs –, squelch if it will
    rain.
A small explosion if it is to be fine.

Our sandwiches are full of sand, but we drink our
    lemonade.
On with our shoes, and we carry our treasures back to
    school.

Jane England

One More Day
(Snapshot haiku)

Sunrise. Alarm clock.
The dark sharp smell of hot toast.
Dress in a hurry.

Kids sauntering past
The usual gang at the gate.
The bell calls us in.

Measuring hands, now.
And I'm looking forward to
Literacy hour,

(Well, sometimes we read
A story or poem that's
Quite interesting).

Big boys and small boys.
Girls chat in groups by the grass.
Thud of a football.

Pizza and baked beans
With long, yellow, half-warmed chips
(We call them bendies).

Huge cardboard cut-out:
I'm painting these monster eyes,
Bloodshot and glaring.

Bullies on the bus.
Then biscuits, sofa, TV.
Supper afterwards.

Bed-time, pyjamas
Quick wash, tingle of toothpaste.
Stare from the window.

When the sky's blackest
And there's not even a moon,
The stars are brightest.

Gerard Benson

June

The Walking Bus

The walking bus goes gliding by
as traffic toots and hoots.
The traffic's stuck. It's nose to tail.
Rows of marching boots
overtake. They're soon ahead,
tramping past at speed
looking like a long and winding
human centipede.

Marian Swinger

Days at School

Like any day
I open our front door.
Against the creosote fence,
Above the clustering pansies
The roses glow dull red;
And further off
Beyond the maple
And the overgrown canal
The orphan hill
That has no name
Rises to the blue.
Like every morning
I stand in the lay-by
In Penthryn Lane
Waiting for the bus.
Proudly Donna tells me,
'I'm going to Honey's house tonight.'
The brakes squeal.
Ann, the driver, wears a boiler suit
And works at Revill's garage in the town.
'Remind your mum
To leave me half a dozen eggs,'
She shouts, her eyes upon the road ahead.

Because it's June and hot today
I sit with Kelly at the back
Beside an open window.
She's not my best friend
But you can always talk to her.
The wind that's blown across the Irish Sea
And half the breadth of Wales
Before rustling our homework books
And my brown hair
Smells hot this day of grass and tar.
Today we're up to Air and Light
In our Jam Jar Science Books.
Later we'll climb on the roof
To drop paper parachutes
On to the playing fields below.
Around the iron gates
The children shout and stare
As we get off the bus.

Gareth Owen

Helen's Lunchbox

I asked Helen,
What have you got in your lunchbox?
She said:

The crunchy taste of a summer orchard
The orange tang of a Spanish holiday
The mooing of cows moving slowly through the grass
The smell of freshly-turned earth
And the salty scent of the sea
All wrapped up
In my mum's warm, morning smile

Roger Stevens

Billy's Lunchbox

I asked Billy,
What have you got in your lunchbox?
Billy said:

An apple
An orange
A squashy banana
A toffee yoghurt
Squeaky mouse crisps
Dragon sausages
A leaky pen
A snail sandwich
An elephant burger
A dinosaur pie
And a giant pumpkin

Would you like a slice?

Roger Stevens

Tent

In my tent
The light is orange.
And I sit here
Still
As if I'm set in jelly.

It's magic here
In this gold space
Where a minute stretches on . . .
  and on . . . and on . . .

Jan Dean

6

When Is a Thing a Living Thing?

If a thing is living it will move
however far or fast or slight,
a falcon swooping on a shrew,
the turning of a leaf to light.

All living things can reproduce,
remake themselves as young and new,
the growing of a rose from seed,
your mother giving birth to you.

A living thing must feed or die
so bats go hunting moths at night,
sheep must graze and insects nibble
and green plants conjure food from light.

And life means growth, things getting bigger,
from tiny sapling to enormous tree,
from foal to horse, from calf to cow,
you, from what you are to what you'll be.

Trevor Parsons

Pupil Troubles

There once was a teacher, Miss Wright,
Whose lessons affected her sight.
    Through all of her classes
    She sported dark glasses –
Her students were simply *too bright*!

Graham Denton

(i) How the light

makes columns dancing dust in the classroom
slants through windows in assembly
fires the trees with green flame
shines on the whiteboard
flickers on and off in the office
polishes the goldfish
makes us blink in the playground
lengthens our shadows by home-time

(ii) How the dark

pools under hanging coats and bags
fills up empty wellingtons
is trapped in the storeroom cupboard
hides behind hands as we count to ten
sleeps inside pencils
falls like curtains in the winter
takes over when we've all gone home

Mandy Coe

Hamster! Hamster!

We've got a hamster in our class
The colour of toffee
It is so sweet, so cute
With chubby cheeks for storing nuts and fruit
It sucks at a water bottle strapped to its cage like a baby
It's soooooo cute,
It's got these darling litte paws
And tiny little tail
Awwwww it is soooooo deliciously cute.

I put my finger up to the cage
And it sniffed it with its adorable chocolate chip nose
And it BIT ME!

We have a hamster in our class
The colour of a bog
It is so mean, so horrible
With fat cheeks for storing pupils' fingers
It sucks at a water bottle strapped to its cage like a greedy
    rat
It's soooooo disgusting,
It's got these vicious little claws
and a long scaly tail
ARRRRR it is soooooo perfectly horrid.

Joseph Coelho

At the End of a School Day

It is the end of a school day
          and down the long driveway
come bag-swinging, shouting children.
          Deafened, the sky winces.
                    The sun gapes in surprise.

190

Suddenly the runners skid to a stop,
      stand still and stare
at a small hedgehog
      curled up on the tarmac
          like an old, frayed cricket ball.

A girl dumps her bag, tiptoes forward
      and gingerly, so gingerly
carries the creature
      to the safety of a shady hedge.
          Then steps back, watching.

Girl, children, sky and sun
      hold their breath.
There is a silence,
      a moment to remember
          on this warm afternoon in June.

Wes Magee

Mrs Mackenzie

Mrs Mackenzie's quite stern.
She says, 'You're not here to have fun,
You're here to learn,'
When I mess about in class.

And in the corridor, if I run
When she's passing by, she shouts
'Slow down! You're not in a race!'
Or 'More haste, less speed!' –
Whatever *that* means.

I never used to like Mrs Mackenzie much.

But the other day
When my dog died
And she saw me crying
She said 'Dogs are such good friends,
Aren't they?'
And she let me stay
In the classroom with her at breaktime
When all the other children went outside
To play.

Mrs Mackenzie's OK.

Gillian Floyd

What For?

We used Pythagoras to build our shed
I needed maths to buy our bread
We used a map to find Aunt Nell's
I caught the bus at half past twelve
My magnet skills found Dad's lost keys
I made a collage of a tree
I took some bottles to the bottle bank
I read a poem to my gran
I helped my mum to bake a cake
I wrote on-line to my friend Kate
I ran and jumped to catch my kite
I sang a song to cheer up Mike
I used old junk to make a rocket
And then used science to try and launch it

Today I really used my brain

Lisa Carter

Literacy Hour

So let's make this clear,
An ADJECTIVE is a
DESCRIBING WORD . . .
(The long, winding, deep, dark, gloomy, secret
Tunnel leads under
The cold, bare, windy, wet, empty
Playground to the
Wild, wonderful, sunny, exciting, outside
World.)

And a NOUN, of course,
Is an OBJECT, a SUBJECT,
A THING . . .
(If only I had
A glider, or a private jet, or a space rocket,
or a hot-air balloon, or a time machine,
I could fly away to
The seaside, or the zoo, or a forest, or Egypt,
or Disneyland, or Anywhere-But-Here.)

A VERB, as we all know,
I hope,
Is a DOING WORD . . .

(I could run, or race, or tiptoe, or clamber,
   or catapult, or dance, or whirl, or just walk
My way to freedom.)

And an ADVERB tells you
Exactly how the action
Is done . . .
(Joyfully, happily, noisily, silently, timidly,
   bravely, desperately, frantically, urgently,
      nervously, wistfully, longingly, dreamily,
Someday,
Sometime,
Soon.)

Clare Bevan

Fellow Suffering

Don't fret if your mum kisses you
in front of your best mate.
His mum's just done the same to him
outside the school yard gate.

Karen Costello-McFeat

The School Boy

I love to rise in a summer morn,
When the birds sing on every tree;
The distant huntsman winds his horn,
And the sky-lark sings with me.
O! what sweet company.

But to go to school in a summer morn,
O! it drives all joy away;
Under a cruel eye outworn.
The little ones spend the day,
In sighing and dismay.

Ah! then at times I drooping sit,
And spend many an anxious hour,
Nor in my book can I take delight,
Nor sit in learnings bower,
Worn thro' with the dreary shower.

How can the bird that is born for joy,
Sit in a cage and sing.
How can a child when fears annoy.
But droop his tender wing.
And forget his youthful spring.

O! father & mother. if buds are nip'd,
And blossoms blown away,
And if the tender plants are strip'd
Of their joy in the springing day,
By sorrow and care's dismay.

How shall the summer arise in joy.
Or the summer fruits appear.
Or how shall we gather what griefs destroy
Or bless the mellowing year.
When the blasts of winter appear.

William Blake

Daisies

Blazing June, dinner-time,
The whole school lazes,
Playfield and lawns
Are white with daisies.

Daisy chains! Let's make
Garlands for teachers!
It might improve
Their hideous features!

What even for Benbow
(Who's always grim)?
Yes, Benbow too –
Especially him.

And so it was made,
Ben's daisy ring:
An airy, fairy
Dare of a thing.

Then the Fearless Two,
Liz and Ted,
Crept up and looped it
Over Ben's head,
And gasped and giggled
And turned and fled.

What then? With the whole school
Holding its breath –
Would Benbow explode?
Cause ruin? Or death?

But no – on his face
Appeared, they say,
A slight, slight smile
That hot June day.

Eric Finney

The Injection

I lined up near the door
Just behind Maggy Moore.
We'd rolled up our sleeves,
And I could see her arm,
All freckly, like Steve's,
And rather thin. *No harm
In asking*, I thought.
So I said, 'Are you scared?'
'A bit,' she said. 'Are you?'
'No,' I said. But I'd been taught not to lie, so I said,
'Well, that's not really true.
I am a bit, too.'

I stood with my arm bared,
And thoughts whizzed round in my head.
One at a time we went in.
'Last of this batch,'
Said the nurse. She rubbed my skin
With something cold. Then, like a pin,
A little sharp scratch.

It didn't really hurt, not much.
Rolling down my sleeve
I went back to our class.
And I was going to sit by Steve,
But there was Maggy in her place,
And to my great surprise
She had tears in her eyes.
'It wasn't as bad as that,'
I said. She burst out crying.
Crying! At her table! In Year Four.

I gave her a gum and sat by her.
Her face was on fire.
'It wasn't really that bad,' she said.
'I was just frightened.' And Miss Lyon
Came over. 'Oh, I'll leave her with you.
You're doing so well . . .' So I sat
By Maggy and we had a chat,
Not much – about this and that.
And that day a silence was broken.
Because I'd never ever spoken
    To Maggy before.

Gerard Benson

A Sense of History

Dry were the words,
dry as the rustling page,
flatly describing extraordinary historical events;
the repeated rebellions of three princes, and
the king their father's dying rage.
The imprisoned queen was a dull figure,
silent actress on a paper stage.

But visiting the real royal castle
on a day trip from school,
metre-thick walls of cold grey stone
jarred imagination. Their senses were stimulated
to a sudden raw grasp of the reality of such rule.
Brutal spiked maces and double-edged swords
brought the youngest prince's cruel
actions frighteningly alive.
They smelled the stench of the midden,
heard squealing pigs and cackling fowl
among hovels hard by the grim defensive walls.
They saw guttering candles in draughty hidden
tower rooms, gloomy and bare, and shuddered
at the thought of being forbidden
ever to leave this damp, unhealthy place.
Ten years a captive guarded here?

Gladly they boarded the coach
for home and modern comforts,
history having momentarily come too near.

Penny Kent

19

Chinese Water Torture

Chinese Water Torture
Drip Drip Drip.
Can I, can I, Mum
Go on the trip trip trip?

Oh can I, Mum? Please let me go. Go on Mum –
Mum . . . pretty please?
I'll even go down on my bended
Knees knees knees.

I'll try wheedling and fawning
From day's end to new day's dawning
I'll work on her all morning.
While she's waking, stretching, yawning.
I will plead and I will beg
Like a cat twined round her leg
Miaowing and miaowing for a feed.

I'll grumble up to bed
My question nagging in her head
Until she sees how very much I NEED.

Oh come on, Mum, I promise
I'll never, never ask,
for a single other thing my whole life long.
But I've really got to do this.
You just don't understand.
To stop me doing this is cruel. It's wrong.
Everyone will be there.
I'll be the only one
The lonely one that's left behind at home.

Can I, can I, Mum,
Go on the trip trip trip?
Chinese Water Torture
Drip Drip Drip.

Jan Dean

Pond Dipping

Blue air above
Blue beating wings
Beneath the shining surface
Wriggling things.
While high in the hedge
A blackbird sings.
Grasses sway
Marsh-Marigolds grow
Here in the meadow
Buttercups glow.
Dip deep
Dip slow
In the smooth green water
Below . . . below.

Jan Dean

Visiting the Castle

We're visiting this castle.
A lot has fallen down.
The slit windows are narrow
for archers to shoot arrows,
and towers watch the town.

There's a gatehouse and portcullis,
some outer walls there too;
and garderobes, the loos
that people had to use,
with holes you could fall through.

We're acting out a story
made up by Mr Wade
in which a loyal knight,
who's been away to fight,
comes back and is betrayed.

A lot of kids are peasants
who tend the stock, of course,
and plough the fields and dig.
Nathaniel is a pig
and Emma is my horse,

while I'm Sir James, the hero.
Serena is my lady.
She overdoes the crying
when she hears I'm dying,
betrayed by Lucas Grady.

But it's not over yet.
Now Serena's choking
while I must lie here dead
with stones under my head –
and this grass which is soaking.

Jill Townsend

When Every Teacher Knows Your Name

He isn't bad; he isn't rude,
He's got what they call 'attitude',
His teachers are, to him, Fair Game
And every last one knows his name.
He isn't rude; he isn't bad,
It's just he likes to drive them mad
By moving when the whistle blows,
By calling out in class,
By pushing into any queue,
Not waiting to be asked.

Yes, every teacher knows his name
Which means he always gets the blame.
The other children point and say,
'*He* did it!' till, when he's away,
They *still* blame him for playing the fool –
Even When He's Not At School!

But that's what happens in this game;
It really drives him wild:
When every teacher knows your name,
So does every child!

Celia Warren

How to Kill a Poet

'The sun is as long as spaghetti' – I said
'No' said Miss Coo 'That can't be right, do it again and do it right'

'Water is as twinkerly as the stars' – I said
'No' said Miss Coo 'That can't be right, do it again and do it right'

'Clouds are fire in the night sky' – I said
'No' said Miss Coo 'That can't be right, do it again and do
   it right'

I wrote a poem for Miss Coo's class . . .

'The sun is round
Water is wet
The clouds are like candy floss.'

I got an A*
And never wrote a poem again.

Joseph Coelho

Do Your Own Thing

Our class had PE in the hall today,
Miss Wells said, 'We're doing dance,
Interpret the music and do your own thing.'
So everyone started to prance.

We fluttered like butterflies, flew like birds,
And some people hovered like bees,
Others were squirrels or tiny wood mice
While some stood and swayed, like the trees.

All of a sudden the music had changed,
It was fast, exciting and loud,
Thunder, lightning and huge drops of rain
Spilling out of a big, black cloud.

The storm was over, the music grew calm,
The rain stopped and out came the sun,
Everyone fluttered or crept once again –
The lesson was so much fun.

Mum came to meet me at half-past three,
As we walked home I started to sing.
'You sound happy,' she said. 'Have you had a good
    day?'
'Oh yes, Mum, we did our own thing.'

Sue Smith

And the Ball Hums

Early we come to school, half washed,
rackets strung, our ankles locked
in regulation shoes and socks.
Girls on a bus with a nosegay of frets,
as criss-cross country roads yawn past,

the year we are mad with summer grass.

Summer grass mown harsh and chalked
with lines and squares containing all:
the rules for nets, for spinning 'starts',
for pairing off, for roles and parts;
all learned by virtue with our hearts;

in spot-lit morning, wait the courts.

The courts beyond the cedar's sway,
whose bulk we seek before the play,
for sweet bark, cool on tender backs.
Hungry for now, and then and next,
we graze together, comparing grips,

until it is time for prettier steps,

Prettier steps walk from the shade,
as butterflies are boldly made.
Shoulders square, our heads side-on,
eyes sharp with stolen breath, held in,
we cast our rude arms to the sun

and the ball hums.

Danielle Sensier

Mouthpiece in a Cluster of Air*

Blood flowing becomes the lungs of Oxen
their external environment a means of receiving
humans through a small hole removing
a low concentration of branches
by which nostrils gather outside the body
Carbo
      carbo
            con
              con
                lary

**A poem of great beauty made by rearranging some of the
words in a baffling science worksheet*

Philip Ardagh

It's Raining on the Trip

It's raining on the trip
Raining on the trip
Drip drip drip
It's raining on the trip.

It's never going to stop
Never going to stop
Drop drop drop
It's never going to stop.

I haven't got a coat
Haven't got a coat
Splish splash splosh
I'm going to get soaked.

Under Ruth's waterproof
Under Pat's pacamac
Under Ella's umbrella
Under Mac's anorak
Things aren't getting much better
Things are getting much wetter

I think it's going to flood
Think it's going to flood
Thud thud thud
I think it's going to flood

The clouds are getting dark
Clouds are getting dark
If it rains much more
Then we're going to need an ark.

Paul Cookson

Dreamer

Often the teacher said, 'Dreamer,
Where is your mind today?'
Got cross sometimes and simply said,
'You'll work while others play.'

But still when the rest were scribbling
And the teacher's tongue was still,
He'd idly gaze through the window
At sun on the singing hill.

And his mind would roam by the mayfield
With the larks all taking flight,
And he'd long to be chasing rabbits
With their tails all flashing white.

Or he'd think of the wooded waters
With the dipper bobbing near,
And he'd long to be plopping pebbles
Where the brook runs fast and clear.

But there's always an end to dreaming –
Or he'd bring on the teacher's rage –
So he'd sigh at the dawdling, crawling clock
And return to the puzzling page.

Eric Finney

Long Division Lesson

Sunil was a quiet child.
No one spoke to him
And he spoke to no one.
Our words jangled around him
Like untuned radios,
While his words whispered secretly

Inside his head.
Only his eyes flashed friendly messages:
'I am not unhappy.'
'I am not afraid of you.'
'I am not completely confused.'

Day after day he watched
While the others talked,
Or dreamed,
Or drew cartoons.
Day after day I scratched pale numbers
On the ghost-grey board.

'Long division,' I said.
'Don't worry if you find it tricky.
Everyone finds it tricky.'
I found it tricky,
So I explained and scratched,
Explained and scratched,
Day after dusty day.

At the end of term,
To test myself,
I tested them.
Only Sunil wrote perfect answers
In perfect, neat rows,
So I rewarded him with the universal language
Of ticks and golden stars,
And he rewarded me with a kindly smile.

Long division lessons can teach us
More than we expect.
Sometimes, for instance,
Numbers speak very clearly
For themselves.
And sometimes even teachers
Are tempted to talk too much.

Clare Bevan

Wilderness

Miss says wilderness
is beautiful, natural, endless . . .
is space.

Gran's Oxford English Dictionary states:
'wild or uncultivated land'.

At the end of our garden
there's a lime tree.
I climb it, high as I can.

Sometimes
I sit up there for hours,
especially in the dark
staring at the stars
touching wilderness

out there
and inside me.

Joan Poulson

July

Changed

For months he taught us, stiff-faced.
His old tweed jacket closely buttoned up,
his gestures careful and deliberate.

We didn't understand what he was teaching us.
It was as if a veil, a gauzy bandage, got between
what he was showing us and what we thought we saw.

He had the air of a gardener, fussily protective
of young seedlings, but we couldn't tell
if he was hiding something or we simply couldn't see it.

At first we noticed there were often scraps of leaves
on the floor where he had stood. Later, thin wisps
of thread like spider's web fell from his jacket.

Finally we grew to understand the work. And on that day
he opened his jacket, which to our surprise
seemed lined with patterned fabric of many shimmering
   hues.

Then he smiled and sighed. And with this movement
the lining rippled and instantly the room was filled
with a flickering storm of swirling butterflies.

Dave Calder

Cinquain

Bully
at the school gates,
fists bunched up like rain clouds
just waiting for the home-time bell
to strike.

Graham Denton

The Trees Behind the Teachers' Cars
Summer Term

Now there's a special new sun-lit green –
a yellowy, mellowy, melt-away green,
like a mermaid, or limeade, or lime marmalade,
or the sheen on Sir's car, now he's had it re-sprayed.
It's a magical green you just glimpse in between,
in long, leafy slithers and thin slitherines,
a sun-shiny shade I've never quite seen,
miracle-made.

Kate Williams

Science Lesson

We've done 'Water' and 'Metals' and 'Plastic',
today it's the turn of 'Elastic':
Sir sets up a test . . .
Wow, that was the best –
he whizzed through the window. Fantastic!

Mike Johnson

The Surprising Number 37

The number 37 has a special magic to it.
If you multiply 37 x 3, you get   111.
If you multiply 37 x 6, you get   222.
If you multiply 37 x 9, you get   333.
If you multiply 37 x 12, you get   444.
If you multiply 37 x 15, you get   555.
If you multiply 37 x 18, you get   666.
If you multiply 37 x 21, you get   777.
If you multiply 37 x 24, you get   888.
If you multiply 37 x 27, you get   999.

Anon.

Summer Fair

No PE today – instead
we are carrying tables onto the field,
putting benches in rows,
marking a pitch for the coconut shy.

Instead of maths, there are numbers on corks –
and if it divides by five
you win a prize.
Boxes and bottles gleam in high piles,
teddy bears wink at packets of sweets.

No literacy hour, but half of Year Six
are printing bright posters,
'Admission 50p.' 'Try your luck.'
'Book bargains here.'

History hovers about the white elephants,
black and white postcards with pictures of trams,
a tortoiseshell hairslide, enormous telephone,
three yellow cups with polkadot saucers.

There are no school dinners in the canteen,
but mountains of cakes, pastel iced,
jewelled with silver balls and Smarties.

Instead of the science topic
there are trays in the corner
full of marigold suns, white bursts of alyssum,
blue lobelia, velvet pansies.

Nobody's thinking of lessons –
even Miss Sefton's smiling,
saying she doesn't think it will rain.

Why can't we do this every week?

Alison Chisholm

Drawer

Don't open Miss MacDonald's drawer
or put your hand inside to get
your confiscated lollipop
catapult or cyberpet.

Behind our toys, the broken chalk,
snapped pencils and bent paper-clips
something strange lurks in the dark –
we're just not sure of what it is.

We've seen Miss slip in crumbs and crusts,
orange peel and apple cores,
we've hears low growls, soft thumping and
the scritch-scratch of tiny sharp claws.

But when we ask her what it is,
Miss smiles – 'It's a dinosaur:
don't you believe me? Just keep your fingers out
– my pet likes to eat them raw.'

Dave Calder

Bug Olympics

We all had competitors ready
In matchboxes, satchels and tins,
Mary-Ann was taking bets on which
Of our creepy-crawlies would win.

The Olympic Committee decided
The race would be run today,
But plans were changed by heavy rain
Which meant an indoor play.

Then Billy's millipede got out
And started across the floor,
So we let all the bugs go
To see who'd be first to the door.

A ladybird took an early lead,
Then a beetle came from the back,
My woodlouse was disqualified
When it fell into a crack.

Miss Crawley came back early,
You should have seen her face,
She turned and ran; we all agreed –
Our teacher won the race.

Robin Mellor

Dear Examiner

Thank you so much for your questions
I've read them all carefully through
But there isn't a single one of them
That I know the answer to.

I've written my name as instructed
Put the year, the month and the day
But after I'd finished doing that
I had nothing further to say.

So I thought I'd write you a letter
Fairly informally
About what's going on in the classroom
And what it's like to be me.

Mandy has written ten pages
But it's probably frightful guff
And Angela Smythe is copying
The answers off her cuff.

Miss Quinlan is marking our homework
The clock keeps ticking away
For anyone not in this classroom
It's just another day.

226

Mother's buying groceries
Grandmother's drinking tea
Unemployed men doing crosswords
Or watching *Crown Court* on TV.

The drizzle has finally stopped here
The sun's just started to shine
And in a back garden in Sefton Road
A housewife hangs shirts on the line.

A class chatters by to play tennis
The cathedral clock has just pealed
A motor chugs steadily back and forth
Mowing the hockey field.

Miss Quinlan's just seen what I've written
Her face is an absolute mask
Before she collects in the papers
I have one little favour to ask.

I thought your questions were lovely
There's only myself to blame
But couldn't you give me something
For writing the date and my name?

Gareth Owen

Last Week of Term and He Wants Us to Write

Sun filters through the window
and clumsily drawn nets.
It is hot on this last week of term
and we don't want to work.
Not today.
Not today when the coming weeks
beckon with opportunity.

We are shown pictures
grainy images of barbed wire
across shrunken faces drawn taut
and he asks us to write
today.
Today when we are looking forward
to our tomorrows.

Rail tracks run to the distance
slowly closing on the narrow point
fading towards the gates of hell
and our tongues struggle with Berkenau
today.
Today when statistics lose any sense
and we no longer comprehend.

John Clarke

Questions

Miss, you ask me questions
But I refuse to crack.
I was always taught that
It's rude to answer back.

Steve Turner

Sports Day

Tomorrow is our school's sports day,
I'm hoping it will rain,
I'm useless at this kind of thing
And don't want to come last again.

Sports day dawns and the sun's out,
There isn't a cloud in the sky,
Looks like sports day is on, then,
'Why couldn't it rain?' I sigh.

Dressed in our shorts and T-shirts
We're all sitting on the grass,
Our mums and dads are watching
So please don't let me come last.

'Skipping race!' calls my teacher,
'Sarah, would you like a go?'
I'm not too bad at skipping,
I wonder if she knows?

I'm standing at the start line
With skipping rope, ready to go,
I'm waiting for the whistle
And hoping I won't be too slow.

The whistle blasts and I'm running,
I fly through my rope so fast,
People are cheering and shouting
And no one's coming past.

I crash through the finishing tape first
And people start patting my back.
'Well done!' 'You won!' 'What a runner!'
'Where did you learn to do that?'

Going home at the end of sports day,
Mum and Dad are oh-so proud.
'You were way ahead,' they tell me,
'Sports day's great!' I shout aloud.

Sue Smith

A Poetry on Geometry

There was once a line
Who was perfectly fine
Till one day she said,
'I need someone, who will be mine.'

So it went out to dine
With another line,
And when they were back
They formed an angle.

'We want to grow'
Said the lines of the angle
'Let's call a third one
And form a triangle.'

A fourth line came in
The triangle to share
And when it joined over
It was a square!

The square was happy
It walked on and on
Till another line joined
To form a pentagon.

When it saw another line
The pentagon said 'Come on'
So when the line joined
It was now a hexagon.

As more lines got added
New shapes were born
Heptagon, octagon, nonagon
And finally a decagon!

With lines and shapes and symmetry,
I made this poetry on Geometry.

Ruhee Parelkar, aged six

The School Band

The one time I played in the school band
They gave me a drum to beat,
'Watch me' said the teacher 'I'll wave my hand.
Meanwhile keep rhythm with your feet.'

Clam-like I held the drum in my knees
And watched every move of her hand,
Waiting for a finger to point at me,
Inviting my turn in the band.

The recorders were playing at full blast,
And the triangles echoed and pinged.
When I thought it was my turn at last
She signalled the choir to sing.

My hand was shaking and ready,
The stick poised at the proper height.
My foot had kept the beat steady,
When my turn came I'd get it right.

The violins squawked their last chords out,
Excitement had made my legs numb.
The choir ended their song with a shout,
But I hadn't yet beaten my drum.

The audience started clapping their hands,
Suddenly it was all over and done.
They applauded the incredible school band,
But I hadn't yet beaten my drum.

So, in that moment of silence
That comes when the clapping ends,
I hit my drum with a violence
That made the drum-stick bend.

I thought that they would do murder,
Then I saw the head teacher come.
My musical career got no further,
For they took away the drum,

And made me sell programmes instead.

Robin Mellor

Writing and Sums

When the teacher asks us to write,
The words dance in my head,
Weaving neat patterns,
Gliding into their places,
Before flowing down my pencil
In an orderly procession
But . . .
When the teacher tells me to do sums,
The figures fly round my head,
Fluttering like birds
Trapped behind glass,
Before escaping down my pencil
In frightened confusion.

John Foster

Last Dive of the Day

You spring into the air
and invert your body,
pierce the water as a herring
gull punctures the ocean.

A perfect dive
and you surface
satisfied

but tense
tense
and taut
as the skin on a drum
your insides churning
mouth desert-dry
and your heart pounding
a thundering beat
you think must be deafening
spectators.

You swim to the pool-side
anxious eyes
scanning the board
search for your score.

Then suddenly
as you heave yourself up
sit
momentarily
on the edge . . .
a cheer.

Narrow-eyed
you make a swift check
then fling back your head
fists in the air
laughing
yelling.

Last dive of the day.
Last year in this school.
And you've won!
The championship
yours.

Grinning
licking and tasting salt
on your face
you fix the lower portion
of your leg in place
and with your heart
now drumming
a stomping song of victory
make your way
to where your family sit
waiting.

Joan Poulson

Moving House

This is the very last day
that I'll be in Class Three.
Tomorrow we're moving away
to a big house near the sea.

I've packed up everything
for the men to put in the van,
but I do wish I could bring
my very best friend Dan.

My new school's really great,
the teacher was kind to me.
The kids all smiled and I can't wait
to see who my friend will be.

'You can have a pet,' says Dad,
'and a slide in the garden too.'
But I still feel a little bit sad,
Dan, who will be playing with you?

Vernon Scannell

Why Are You Late for School?

I didn't get up
because I was too tired
and I was too tired
because I went to bed late
and I went to bed late
because I had homework
and I had homework
because the teacher made me
and the teacher made me
because I didn't understand
and I didn't understand
because I wasn't listening
and I wasn't listening

because I was staring out of the window
and I was staring out of the window
because I saw a cloud.
I am late, sir,
because I saw a cloud.

Steve Turner

Tall Story

graph

m_y
on
it
fit
not
could
but
giraffe,
a
measure
to
went
I went to measure a giraffe, but could not fit it on my

Mike Johnson

At the School Camp

In our hut, I'm first awake.
I peer through the curtains –
nothing's stirring out there
except for three blackbirds and a crow
looking for their breakfast – maybe a worm
or two. Haven't they slept? It's only six o'clock!
Everyone in this hut is still asleep.

Then suddenly I see the sun
climbing, climbing, ever so slowly –
a faraway orange
that I can't reach.

Katherine Gallagher

Presentation Day

Everyone was nervous about reading out their poems.
We had trouble even getting Richard on stage.
They went up and read so quietly we couldn't hear.
'Speak up, dear,' tried a mum.
The parents sat in the crowd,
Smiling and encouraging.
Then it was the students' turn to read.
I don't know why all the teachers had so much trouble.

Celina Macdonald

What Book Am I?

Turn my pages, reader.
I am no ordinary book,
I am not a storyteller,
yet worth your long hard look.

An armchair traveller
can climb my mountains, swim my seas,
marvel at the range I cover,
visit many countries.

I am well named after
a giant who shouldered the Earth.
Geography holds no terror;
in me it takes its birth.

Debjani Chatterjee

answer: Atlas

It's Only a Matter of Time

One day she's going to ask me.
Not today
or tomorrow. But soon.
It's only a matter of time
before I'll be walking out of the room,

and I'll close the door behind me
and I'll creep down the corridor
and I'll skate into the assembly hall
(on the flippery-slippery floor)
and I'll look straight up at the big wall clock
and her words will tick in my ears:

Jamie Brock,
go and look at the clock
and tell me what's the time.

And that's when it will happen; my brain
will turn to mush, while big hands join
with little hands
and numbers mix and match.

Everyone else in class, I know,
has been telling the time for years;
the scary, secret language
of seconds and minutes and hours.
Next, it's Sally Barker's turn,
so after, it must be mine.
She's working her way through the register.
It's only a matter of time.

Danielle Sensier

The Truant's School Report

Shy
Could do better
Handwriting needs improving
Occasionally daydreams
Odd one out in class
Loner

Runs in the corridors
Economical with the truth
Punishment cuts no ice
Often conspicuous by absence
Rebel without a cause
Thank goodness term's over!

Debjani Chatterjee

Speech Day at Mount Augustine's in the Fields

blah blah blah blah blah blah blah blah
blah blah . . . governors . . . blah blah blah
blah . . . new . . . blah blah . . . building plans . . . blah
  blah
blah blah . . . achievements . . . blah blah
blah blah . . . endeavour . . . blah blah blah
blah blah blah . . . Mount Augustine spirit . . . blah blah
blah blah blah . . . extraordinary . . . blah blah
blah blah . . . disturbances . . . blah blah blah
blah blah . . . *sheep* . . . blah blah blah
. . . quivering . . . blah blah blah . . . baaaaaa!
blah blah . . . eco garden . . . blah blah blah
blah blah blah . . . heads . . . blah blah . . . off gnomes . . .
blah blah . . . lights . . . blah blah . . . over new mobile . . .
  blah blah
blah blah blah . . . year five . . . blah blah
blah blah . . . teleported . . . blah blah blah
blah . . . experiments . . . blah blah blah . . . hideous . . .
  blah
blah blah blah blah . . . bright side . . . blah
blah . . . positive . . . blah blah . . . outcome . . . blah blah

blah blah blah . . . smaller class sizes . . . blah blah
blah . . . teacher/pupil ratio . . . blah blah blah
blah blah . . . Ofsted . . . blah blah blah.

Sports day!
blah blah
blah blah blah blah
blah blah blah
blah blah blah blah blah blah
blah blah blah blah blah blah blah . . .

Chris d'Lacey

We Lost Our Teacher to the Sea

We've been at the seaside all day
collecting shells, drawing the view
doing science in the rockpools.

Our teacher went to find the sea's edge,
and stayed there, he's sitting on a rock
he won't come back.

His glasses are frosted over with salt
his beard has knotted into seaweed
his black suit is covered in limpets.

He's staring into the wild water
singing to the waves
sharing a joke with the herring gulls.

We sent out the coastguard
the lifeboat and the orange helicopter
he told them all to go away.

We're getting on the bus with our sticks of rock
our presents for Mum
and our jotters and pencils.

He's still out there as we leave
arms outstretched to the pale blue sky
the tide racing towards him.

His slippery fishtail flaps
with a flick and a shimmer he's gone
back to the sea for ever.

David Harmer

Two Times Table

Twice one are two,
Violets white and blue.

Twice two are four,
Sunflowers at the door.

Twice three are six,
Sweet peas on their sticks.

Twice four are eight,
Poppies at the gate.

Twice five are ten,
Pansies bloom again.

Twice six are twelve,
Pinks for those who delve.

Twice seven are fourteen,
Flowers of the runner bean.

Twice eight are sixteen,
Clinging ivy ever green.

Twice nine are eighteen,
Purple thistles to be seen.

Twice ten are twenty,
Hollyhocks in plenty.

Twice eleven are twenty-two,
Daisies wet with morning dew.

Twice twelve are twenty-four,
Roses . . . who could ask for more.

Anon.

Words Are Magic

Words are magic
    you can pluck new ones
    from the air:
        popple
        chopswaffle

or share old ones in games:
        The farmer's in his den
        The farmer's in his den
        Eeh Aye Adee Oh
        The farmer's in his den

become excited by rich words
from other lands:
> *Shanthi*
> *Nama*

choose funny words
as names for each other
or for a gloopy baby brother

discover powerful words
in dictionaries:
> *unity*
> *autonomy*

on

find the wonder of words   on
in a story that's scary
or one that makes you laugh
until you cry   on

explore new worlds in words
when you write a poem
of your own.   on

Yes! Words are fun
and words can bite.   on

Words are magic
> that goes on   on
>   on
> and on
>   forever

Joan Poulson

Nearly

Half an hour to go
Each tick of the clock
Kicks the second hand
Closer to home time.

Sunlight streams
Down half-open windows,
Halfway home
Our thoughts scatter.

To perfect beaches in the sun
Swimming pools and aeroplanes
Busy cities far away
Country lanes, long green hills.
Endless hours of nothing.

Ten minutes to go
We hold our breath
The classroom clock
Clears its throat.

Crams more minutes
In its tick-tock mouth
Swallows hard,
Thirty seconds left.

David Harmer

The Sunshine of Susan Browne

Heat melts and curls things blackly.
Ice burns your skin, hurts your teeth.
Susan Browne understands these things.
She counts stars – gives new ones names.

Today she learned about the footprints
of dinosaurs. Last week she discovered
the heart of a flower looks like a cathedral.
She measures water in a beaker.
She sifts sand and smiles.

Through the microscope,
ants are giants; feathers are forests;
sugar is snow. And inside Susan Browne
swirls a galaxy of questions, curiosity
making her shine like a sun.

Mandy Coe

31

Late July

What happens when the gates are locked
and summer starts, beyond the playground's
chain-link fence, that famous puddle
dry in the centre circle, and blades of grass
back in the goalmouths worn to mud
all term, a solitary sick-note
fading on a staffroom window sill,
the registers completed for another year?

The long days hang from us like stones.
They drag us to the earth. They make us sleep.
And while we sleep, our voices break,
our faces change, our clothes tear at the seams.
We are lost in fields, in woods, in towns.
We will never be the same again.

Stephen Knight

August

Prayer for the First Day of the School Holidays

Dear God . . . please . . .

Let rain be banished and the sun be strong
Let time pass slowly and the days be long

Let laughter echo forever with friends
Let fun and games be without end

May good days be many and bad days be few
May parents not find odd jobs for you

May bikes be indestructible and balls not be lost
May day trips be bountiful whatever the cost

May school be something we never remember
Let it always be August and never September

Thanks
Amen

Paul Cookson

On the First Day of the Summer Holidays

Lie in bed late
　　　　lounging and lolling about
Eat eggs and bacon
　　　　for breakfast at eleven

Sprawl on the lawn
　　　　with a long glass of lemonade
And eat salad and seafood
　　　　Travel the town T-shirted

Greeting mates
       grinning with freedom Bowl
Bash those bails down
       Belt a leather ball

Bouncing to the boundary bounce bounce
       Bring
A take-away home
       parathas and popadums

Talk about treats
       sunlight through trees and sand
Sleep in deep silence between sheets
       Dream

Fred Sedgwick

Holidays: Day 3

There's a lovely smell from the kitchen,
and a banging in my head
from my brother's bedroom
as I lie in bed.

It's the third day of the hols.
Nothing to do all day
but talk to friends and Granny
or go outside and play.

The only history
is what we did last week.
Geography is finding
a place for hide and seek.

No stories to write down:
we'll act them all instead.
I'll be a wartime hero.
My HQ is the shed.

Or I could be a spaceman
jumping around on the moon,
or maybe a zookeeper
playing with a baboon.

Perhaps I'll stay in bed though.
Well, I would if I could
but oh, my tummy's rumbling
and breakfast smells so good.

Jill Townsend

Holiday Diary

On the first day of the holidays
My mother said to me:
'Clear out your disgusting bedroom.'

On the second day of the holidays
My mother said to me:
'Help with the washing up and
Clear out your disgusting bedroom.'

On the third day of the holidays
My mother said to me:
'Do some weeding in the garden,
Help with the washing up and
Clear out your disgusting bedroom.'

On the fourth day of the holidays
My mother said to me:
'Take your brother to the park,
Do some weeding in the garden,
Help with the washing up and
Clear out your disgusting bedroom.'

On the fifth day of the holidays
My mother said to me:
'Go to the shops for me and
Take your brother to the park,
Do some weeding in the garden,
Help with the washing up and
Clear out your disgusting bedroom.'

On the sixth day of the holidays
I said, 'Can I go back to school?'

Trevor Millum

Teacher Next Door!

Today we're going on holiday,
My mum and dad and my sister, Fay,
We're going to France to stay in a tent,
We have to catch a ferry from Kent.

When we arrive at our campsite
We look at our tent, so big and bright,
The sun is out, it's a lovely day,
This will be a brilliant holiday!

Once we've had tea at a table outside
We play hide-and-seek and it's Fay's turn to hide.
I count to a hundred, look round – I'm sure
That's my teacher right next door!

I cannot think of a word to say,
I can't believe that we've come all this way
To find my teacher staying next door –
I go all shy and look down at the floor.

'Hello,' she says. 'This is a surprise!'
From inside her tent someone suddenly cries.
She's here with her husband and, what's more,
She's got two children of six and four.

My shyness doesn't last very long,
She doesn't care if I do something wrong,
She's on holiday, too, and what's really cool
Is she hardly ever mentions school.

What a great holiday! So much fun,
With lots to do and plenty of sun,
Her children are cute and seem to like us
And one day, while we're out, we meet on a bus.

It all ends too soon and we're back at home,
It's strange now she's gone, I feel somehow alone
Till I call my friends, saying: 'Guess who I saw,
Our teacher was in the tent next door!'

Sue Smith

Holidays

Happy-go-lucky days.
Off out and about days.
Lazy lie-in-bed days.
In front of TV days.
Do as you please days.
Away to the sea days.
You can choose what to do days.
School's over! We're free days!

John Foster

Not Only Pebbles
(a guide for young beachcombers)

With school holidays just round the corner,
and with summer stretched out like a dancer,
now – as parents discuss the main fortnight:
'To the seaside!' most children will answer.

Come the day, all excited and breathless,
down the rocks to the shore you will clamber,
where – among larger stones mostly worthless –
with luck you may find precious amber.

Spreading out, then, along the white beaches,
you may spot a huge crab in a rock-pool,
or – magically, buried in seaweed –
the toy that you once lost in Blackpool.

Chances are that, while stopping for ice-cream,
one day, by an old ruined castle,
you'll find something rather exciting,
inside a silk purse with a tassel.

Your creative skills, too, may be tested:
by an empty boat . . . going full throttle;
by the sight of an SOS message,
right there, at your feet, in a bottle!

Yes, a beachcomber's life can be lovely,
with amber from Southwold to pocket,
plus winkles to pick in Clovelly,
for you to sell, straight from the bucket.

So, good luck on your seaside adventures,
as you bring home a fortune, m'hearties,
or – woefully – nothing more precious
than . . . a sad-looking tube of wet Smarties!

Monica Hoyer

Arithmetic

She takes ten and divides it by three:
it breaks, hard-edged, echoing.

She divides a wet sky by a high window,
she wants to add a radio, take away the teacher.
The day isn't working out right.

She's given up caring about correct answers.
That makes the sums easy. So easy it bores her.

She measures the drawn-out length of the lesson
against the chipped edge of the desk – and still
finds it's too long till the bell.

She counts up her friends and subtracts
her enemies. Now that's interesting

but difficult, difficult.

Dave Calder

9

Potions

For warm summer weather
mix a potion of Dandelion and Heather.

For everlasting sweets
mix a potion of Wisteria and beets.

For exploring a forest path
mix a potion of bark and rotten leaf.

For days off school, and playing in snow
mix a potion of Hawthorn and Sloe.

For winter days to pass
mix a potion of Night Shade and frosted grass.

To disappear without a trace
mix a potion of Old Man's Beard and Mace.

To finally get your own room
mix a potion of Rose and Lemon Balm.

For late nights, TV, and staying up
mix a potion of Daffodil and Buttercup.

If you plan to run away
mix a potion of sedge and hay.

But if you're ready to come back home
mix some Snowdrop and Teasel comb.

To just sit and be your very own age
plant Forget-me-nots and Sage.

Michael Kavanagh

Waiting for the Start of Term

Early August
And the school is silent.
Along each empty corridor
No footsteps come clattering
And the chattering
Of children's voices can't be heard.
Only shadows move across the empty hall
And, on the wall,
The clock ticks down each minute, hour, day
Since everybody went away.

It's summertime
But in the school a sort of gloom
Hangs in the air,
A sadness that nobody's there.
Computer screens gaze at each other blankly
And chairs, unsat-on,
Stand awkwardly about in every room.
Everything seems stunned
By so much absence . . . for what's a school
Without teachers and pupils?
And so it waits for the moment when
Life returns to it once again.

Gillian Floyd

She Sells Sea-Shells

She sells sea-shells on the sea shore;
The shells that she sells are sea-shells I'm sure.
So if she sells sea-shells on the sea shore,
I'm sure that the shells are sea-shore shells.

Anon.

On a Blue Day

On a blue day
when the brown heat
scorches the grass
and stings my legs with sweat

I go running like a fool
up the hill towards the trees
and my heart beats loudly
like a kettle boiling dry.

I need a bucket the size of the sky
filled with cool, cascading water.

At evening
the cool air rubs my back
I listen to the bees
working for their honey

and the sunset pours light
over my head like a waterfall.

David Harmer

Little Silver Aeroplane

Little silver aeroplane
Up in the sky,
Where are you going to
Flying so high?
Over the mountains
Over the sea
Little silver aeroplane
Please take me.

Anon.

Grandad's Garden

is heady with perfumes,
wallflowers, carnations,
velvet roses, lilac.

All the bees get tipsy.

He wins prizes. There are
cups, shields around the clock
on the sideboard.

Grandma polishes them
with yellow dusters.

Grandad shows his garden to me
every Sunday. Sweet peas
like bright butterflies,
sky-blue scabious,
the fairy hats of columbines.

His garden is a place
(listen to those ring-a-ding
Canterbury bells!)
that's telling you

what wonderful things
love can do.

Matt Simpson

The Swing

How do you like to go up in a swing,
　Up in the air so blue?
Oh, I do think it the pleasantest thing
　Ever a child can do!

Up in the air and over the wall,
　Till I can see so wide,
Rivers and trees and cattle and all
　Over the countryside –

Till I look down on the garden green,
　Down on the roof so brown –
Up in the air I go flying again,
　Up in the air and down!

Robert Louis Stevenson

Where Is Everybody?

Here we are, two weeks into the summer holidays,
and there's no one around. It's not
like Alasdair who went to Loch Ard
or Cafy who went to Iran
and never came back. It's not
even like Ola who went to Bearsden
or Emma who changed schools
and were hardly seen again.
It's not even like Cassy whose mum's
full of twins and moving house.
I can understand them. It's life.
People move.
But this is strange – there's
no one. I go to the supermarket, to the park,
and there's no one I even know. I ring their bells,
I ring them up – no one answers. They can't
all be away. It's as if they'd all gone
on holiday together, to a party without inviting me.
I play with this and that, I watch telly, read comics,
sometimes go swimming or get taken places.

I even play with toddlers. I go to the gardens,
kick a ball, hide in trees.
But there's a big hole inside me. I keep
expecting my friends to jump from the bushes
shouting surprise. I wonder
who'll be there when school starts again.
Will I be in a class of one?

Dave Calder

Beach for Ruksar

This beach has blonde sand sieved as fine as flour,
pebbles in sixteen shades of blue,
smooth black rock which shines with every tide.

Lines of limpets shelter in the cracks,
a pool appears with waving crabs and swaying weed.
There's bladder wrack and razor shells,
and waves which rise and crash
and bubble to the shore.

At first the sea feels icy cold,
you scream and run away.
'Come back Ruksar,' it says to you,
'Try again, be bold.'

You teeter on the edge a while
then stretch your arms and launch into the surf.
Your eyes are bright,
you smile out loud,
your body shakes with a watery laugh.

Chrissie Gittins

Summer at Granny's House

It's so annoying going to bed when it's LIGHT!

If I got up and opened the curtain
I would see my granny's green car.
She spilt a thing of milk in it two years ago.
On hot days it still smells of sick.

If I opened the window now
I would hear the distant roar of the motorway,
the nearer roar of the lawn mower,
the wind caught in the black Maple tree.

If I went down and opened the door
I would smell the blossoms that only grow
on this street, a scent like candy floss.
The cut grass, and the smell of wet tar.

If I went out and walked
I would feel the sun melting on my skin,
my face itchy from swimming pool water,
and the pricks of grass poking up through my pyjamas.

I'd walk to the hammock, and lie down there
with its mildewy rope on my back.
Tomorrow we'll swim again and it will be hot.
Grass cuttings will stick to our feet. It will be great!

But for now, I HATE going to bed in the light.

Michael Kavanagh

Teachers' Holidays

Mr Mason flies
to Tenerife. Lies
lazy in the sun.
Eats out, no grief.

The Head would
rather exercise.
Climbing mountains
Under cloudy skies.

Mrs Clancy's family
goes to France.
Camping.
Nothing fancy.

Bognor's Mrs Major's
destination.
(Not gifted with
imagination.)

But our Miss Drew!
Backpacks her way to
distant Kathmandu.
Wish we could too!

Ann Bonner

Towards the End of Summer

Cherry red and honey bee
Buzzed around the Summer flowers
Bumbled round the luscious fruits.
Patient weaver clambered by

Silently while the others bobbed
And busied in the bright blue air
Hither, zither, merrily,
Weaver waved his cool brown arms
And gently drew around the tree
Silken skeins so fine so fine
No one could see that they were there,
Until one Autumn morning when
Cherry was gone and bee asleep
A silver shawl was laced across the grass
With little beads like pearls strung all along.

Jenny Joseph

Starfish and Other Shapes

If I had to choose a shape,
I think the one the starfish has is best,
with five arms, or more,
and a mouth at the centre of myself!

I could live in a tangle of seaweed,
or like the reflection
of a fallen star,
be seen floating in rock pools.

As a globe-shaped sea-urchin,
with long, smooth spines,
I could live on the lower shore
under a cluster of stones.

If I chose to be leaf-shaped,
like the flat sea worm, I could glide
through the waves. Or, as a round,
red, ribbon worm, I might burrow in sand.

If I kept on swimming, I might resemble
the pen-like shape of a common squid,
or take on the umbrella look
of a floating jellyfish!

I still think that to be shaped like a star
would be fun,
yet I cannot imagine being any shape
but the one I am!

Doris Corti

What We Did on Our Holidays

Miss Moss asked us
What we did on our holidays
And Billy said

He went to Mars
In a spaceship

Miss Moss said
Are you certain you went to Mars?
And Billy said
It may have been Margate

Miss Moss said
Are you certain you went in a spaceship?
And Billy said
It may have been a bus

Miss Moss said
What did you do in Margate?
And Billy said
We had to fight the aliens
To rescue the princess
From the terrifying monster

Miss Moss said
Did anyone else
Do anything interesting
On their holiday?

Roger Stevens

Turning Over

The first page of my new workbook
Is smooth and plump
Cushioned by all the other pages of the book.
When I write on it,
I love the way my pen glides.
I love the flow of it,
The fluid slow and gentle slide of it,
The fat and massy paper underside of it.
Writing then is bliss,
But this – this second page is not.
The hard card of the cover
Feels thin and scribbly
And my pen scratches like a cat claw.
I would like to make a law
Against second pages.

Jan Dean

Ms Fleur

Though she doesn't know it,
Our teacher is a mermaid.
We built her from Skegness sand,
Me and Emily,
Sculpted a swishing tail,
Curved scales with the edge of our hands,
And arranged her driftwood hair in a spiky halo.

All day we piled the sand and patted her.

Though she didn't see it,
We wrote her name, Ms Fleur,
In our biggest letters,
Me and Emily,
Next to her blue shell belly button,
And her squidgy seaweed earrings
That popped between our fingers.

All day we piled the sand and patted her.

Though she didn't hear it,
We sang a mermaid song,
And screeched like seagulls,
Me and Emily,
As we fixed her fins,
And tiny pebble eyes,
Saw crabs scuttle across her shingle necklace.

All day we piled the sand and patted her.

Until finally the sea lapped at her fins,
Her driftwood hair, her seaweed earrings,
And she swished her fish tail,
High into the foam,
Calling,
'Katie, Emily,
It's time to go,
It's time for home,
It's time to say goodbye you know!'

Mary Green

Limpet

I am a Cornish limpet,
  been here for a hundred years,
    sucking and gripping and sticking to this stone
    with a hundred thousand fears.

    What if I get put in a bucket
      and dumped in the boot of a car,
        with wellies and jellies and a windbreaker
        and a shell in the shape of a star?

      I'd miss my chats with the ancient crab,
      the swell and wash of the tide,
        the soothing stroke of anemones,
          the storms when the fish come and hide.

        But I hang on tight and hope for the best,
        I avoid anyone with a spade,
          when the sun beats down in a glisten
          on the sea, my fears begin to fade.

Chrissie Gittins

The End of the Holidays

Too hot, too close
with the grumbling rumble of thunder,
last night was no night for sleep.
And this morning, purple black clouds
with low insistent murmur,
sweep over peaks and circulate the valley.
For two weeks, cosseted and creamed
our Anglo-Saxon skin has braved the bullying sun,
our tongues have rehearsed polite conventions
and we've gasped at the speed of response.
We've done our best, not wishing to be
archetypal monoglots
but (and sorry to take this personal)
with a season's switch change overnight,
the need now for a warmer sweater
and the repeated rumbling refrain,
the message is clear:
it's time to go home.

John Clarke

It's Not What I'm Used To

I don't want to go to Juniors . . .

The chairs are too big.
I like my chair small, so I fit
Exactly
And my knees go
Just so
Under the table.

And that's another thing –
The tables are too big.
I like my table to be
Right
For me
So my workbook opens
Properly.
And my pencil lies in the space at the top
The way my thin cat stretches into a long line
On the hearth at home.

Pencils – there's another other thing.
Another problem.
Up in Juniors they use pens and ink.
I shall really have to think

About ink.

Jan Dean

Nature Table

I'll bring in a yellow flower
With its face turned to the sky

I'll bring in cool rain
For the thirsty earth

I'll bring in late sunshine
And stars at midnight in June

I'll bring in a reed
To sing of wet places

I'll bring in the sand between my toes
From a long hot summer

287

I'll bring in a white cloud
To lower the sky

I'll bring in a twig
That remembers a storm

I'll bring in a holly bush
With the sharp breath of winter

I'll bring in a sleeping bulb
With the promise of spring.

Lucinda Jacob

Memories of Schooldays
(a sedoka*)

As we were best friends
we enrolled in the same school
and took part in the same games.

Now as we look back,
how is it our memories
of schooldays are not the same?

Debjani Chatterjee

* *A sedoka is a form of Japanese poetry with six lines in two halves and a syllable count of 5–7–7 and 5–7–7. The second half retains the theme but represents a shift in perspective.*

30

Quieter Than Snow

I went to school a day too soon
And couldn't understand
Why silence hung in the yard like sheets
Nothing to flap or spin, no creaks
Or shocks of voices, only air.

And the carpark empty of teachers' cars
Only the first September leaves
Dropping like paper. No racks of bikes
No kicking legs, no fights,
No voices, laughter, anything.

Yet the door was open. My feet
Sucked down the corridor. My reflection
Walked with me past the hall.
My classroom smelt of nothing. And the silence
Rolled like thunder in my ears.

At every desk a still child stared at me
Teachers walked through walls and back again
Cupboard doors swung open, and out crept
More silent children, and still more.
They tiptoed round me
Touched me with cold hands
And opened their mouths with laughter that was

Quieter than snow.

Berlie Doherty

School Holiday Blues

From our empty classroom escapes a little sigh
as if it really misses having children passing by.
Its desktops look so lonely, they smell alien and
clean. The bin is black and sullen, no litter to be
seen, the numbers sit in silence refusing to add up
between the mournful pencils and unread reading
books. Pens stand
to attention, chairs
all wait in line. The only property is lost
an unwatched clock marks time. There's
only one sad trainer and an empty pencil
case, hanging off
the coat pegs; our
hall is just a space
and outside in the
playground, birds
with no snacks to
eat, watch an old
grey ball, moved **eet.**
along by unseen

Sue Hardy-Dawson

September

Going to Secondary

The summer holidays are almost over.
Everyone's been on holiday
and come back sun-tanned.
Children sleep late then play all day.

Each early morning is misty and chilled,
as if the season has become fed up with
the same old hot days and wants a change.

In just four days' time I shall be going
to secondary school.
I have never been as excited as this!

My new uniform hangs in the wardrobe
and every now and again, I wander upstairs
pretending I'm going to read a book or something,
but really I just want to look at my new uniform.

I run my fingers across the yellow
diagonal stripes on my black tie,
or try on my black jacket
(it's just a little too long in the sleeves,
but my Mum says it's got to last a few years).
I am really looking forward to putting it on
and walking with my friends to secondary school
in the cool, morning sunshine.

My friends! Of course!
I can't wait to see my friends
in *their* uniforms! No more little
blue jumpers like we wore in primary!
No more boring clothes and shoes with buckles,
we're going to wear slip-ons and the latest fashions.

Only four days to go and I'll be
at secondary school. I feel like the
whole world is hurtling and spinning
and zooming and changing –
and me, little me, I'm right in the middle of it!
What if I get lost in that huge school?
It's vast and maze-like with hundreds
of corridors and classes.
What if I'm late on the very first day – oh no!

Mum says we'll go into town on Monday morning
and get my shoes, and then that's it –
I'll be ready!
(What if they don't have my size?)

I'm so excited and then again,
I'm so nervous and anxious!
Only four more days,
four more days and I'll be
at secondary school.

Say goodbye to childhood for me.

John Rice

I Am Full of Promise

The sky at dusk has changed from dove to slate,
the nights are closing in and turning cool.
The thrill of autumn promises awaits:
tomorrow is my first day back at school.
My teachers will remember me I'm sure
and not for any naughtiness – not me.
The dinner ladies know I don't eat chips –
I need pure protein for my GCSE's.
And if I live in dread of those exams
and if I doubt my popularity
or luck with boys, proficiency at sport,
I still enjoy the possibility
that I am full of promise like the autumn.
I'll love my GCSE's when I've got 'em.

Linda Lee Welch

3

Prayer for the Last Day of the School Holidays

Dear God
Thank you for the holidays, the sun and the shine
But if it's OK with you, can you please stop time?

May the school be closed and the staff be away
And please can we have just one more day?

And if you can't do these then please may it rain
So we don't feel bad about school time again

Thanks
Amen

Paul Cookson

Frog Class

I am in Frog Class
Ugly old Frog Class
Not Cat Class
Or Dog Class
But drippy old Frog Class

There's Antelope
And Elephant
And Leopard-with-his-spots Class
And Dragon Class
Flamingo Class
And clever, crafty Fox Class

But I am in Frog Class
The hide-in-the-grass class
The croak class
The joke class
Oh why am I in Frog Class?

Roger Stevens

New Boy

Today
everyone is laughing
at your long name
and your skinny legs
which look like
two burnt-out matches
but by next week
I bet
they'll be your friends.

Pauline Stewart

Mum's Umbrage

The teacher called my mother,
on my first day back at school –
he told her I'd been naughty,
and behaving like a fool.

'Now just you wait a minute,'
came my mother's quick response,
'he misbehaved all summer
and I never called *you* once!'

Graham Denton

Our Claire

My sister goes to big school every day.
Her uniform is smart; she wears a tie.
As she boards the bus she seems to say
I'm cool, I'm smart, I never need to cry.
Her school bag's stuffed with lots of different things.
Her homework's neatly done and marked with ticks.
She knows about volcanoes, sums and kings.
She makes me smile by telling me of tricks
that naughty children play on all the staff
like passing notes around in lesson time.
My clever sister often makes me laugh
and helps me do my schoolwork, like this rhyme.
In just a few more years I'll be like her.
You'd really like my sister, our Claire.

Angela Topping

The Size of the Problem

High school
looks so big
Infants and juniors so . . . small
There are so many pupils lots of them. Everywhere. Out
   there, running
about in the yard. In here, filling up all of the classrooms.
   There are
just
hundreds and
      hundreds and
            hundreds and
                  hundreds and
hundreds and
      hundreds and
            hundreds and
                  hundreds and
hundreds and
      hundreds and
            hundreds and
                  hundreds of people
                        everywhere.

In primary school there were
      just a few of us.

Tony Bower

Special to Me

He was lean and neat and wrinkled
Like a flag that's freshly furled.
His voice was strained through years of pain
But he opened up my world.

He helped me overcome my fear
Of numbers and the sums I wrote,
Inspired in me a love of words
That I could use like 'anecdote'.

He stirred in me a light to see
The secret underworld of seed,
Of snails and insects, spawn in streams,
The need of life to feed and breed.

He taught me how to draw and paint,
To see afresh the world around,
Encouraged all experiment
In music and the joy of sound.

He's now forgotten, long retired
But he was special then to me.
The light is brighter, grass more green,
Because he taught me how to see.

Jane Mann

The Football Team

Number One
Here we come
Number Two
White and Blue
Number Three
Pass to me
Number Four
I'm going to score
Number Five
Goalie's dive
Number Six
Striker's tricks
Number Seven
I can head them
Number Eight
Shot too late

Number Nine
That ball's mine
Number Ten
Shoot again
Number Eleven
It's a goal
Celebrate
With a forward roll

Roger Stevens

Me & You

The long-legged girl who takes goal-kicks
is me.
I loop my 'j' and 'g's,
twiddle my hair
and wobbled a loose tooth
through History all yesterday afternoon.

The small shy boy who draws dragons
is you.
You can multiply,
make delicious cheese scones
and when my tooth finally

falls out and I cry in surprise,
you hand me a crumpled tissue.

I will be an Olympic athlete,
win two bronze medals.
You will be a vet with gentle hands
who gets cats to purr and budgies speak.

We don't know this yet
but we will be each other's first date.
One kiss.
That's all . . . but
for the rest of our lives we never, ever forget.

In the meantime,
my tongue explores the toothless gap
and you lean over your desk and concentrate
on drawing the feathery,
feathery lines of a dragon's wings.

Mandy Coe

Dress Sense

You shoulda seen the new teacher
by the way,
pure crazy looking so he wiz.

He hud a mad ponytail
tied wi a kinda elastic band
so he did.

An these pure crazy
purple-tintit glasses,
and this tartan waistcoat,
pure bright silky like,
the whole class wiz blinded by it
so they wur.

It was pure whoaaaaaaaaawee!

Then this green jaiket
with rid bits aw ower it
the kind you widnae be seen dead in
by the way.

Then his Doc Marten boots
with the wee totey labels
looked stupit so they did.

An he pure takes oot
wan ae they luminous watches
by the way.

Then *he* tells *us*
tae pay attention
and I hud to look the other way
at Julie
who was pure guttin hersel
by the way
. . . pure guttin hersel.

Brian Whittingham

The Trees Behind the Teachers' Cars
Autumn Term

Behind the cars the trees have turned to treasure –
red as rubies, gold as gold bars.

If Sir was a pirate
he'd be cramming his boot with booty,
except that it's really just leaves, of course,
gone bizarre.

Kate Williams

Magnify

Under the glass eye
moth's wing
spread.

Tapestry
of tiny stitches:
cinnamon, cream, magenta red.

Gossamer threads
in perfect place.
Magic carpet.

Joan Poulson

The Music Lesson Rap

I'm the bongo kid,
I'm the big-drum-beater,
I'm the click-your-sticks,
I'm the tap-your-feeter.
When the lesson starts,
When we clap our hands,
Then it's me who dreams
Of the boom-boom bands,
And it's me who stamps,
And it's me who yells
For the biff-bang gong,
Or the ding-dong bells,
Or the cymbals (large),
Or the cymbals (small),
Or the tubes that chime
Round the bash-crash hall,
Or the tambourine,
Or the thunder-maker –
But all you give me
Is the sssh-sssh shaker!

Clare Bevan

Moonwatch

We're studying the moon –
drawing it, remembering all the moons
we've ever seen.

Just now, through the window,
there's a daylight-moon looking fragile,
egg-shell soft.

I've no plans to go up there
whizzing through the blue,
blasting into space.

And I can't stop thinking
about a blood-orange full moon
I saw inching up

into the summer sky in France.
It moved so slowly,
became a golden balloon

that never hurried.
I wanted to follow it,
catch it. But I never did.

Katherine Gallagher

Assembly (Haiku)

The Head is giving
assembly today. Let's pray
he's little to say.

Ann Bonner

Melting Pot
(With thanks to Simon Armitage)

Formula and periodic
elemental table, changing states
class 3B in the crucible
transformation waits.

Among a group of stupid boys
you, calling me by name
passing me the scissors
heated on a flame.

A frog for the kissing
but now I sit and wince
about paying you attention
my embryonic prince.

No place for alchemy
a lesson sadly learned
still ready to forgive
but I'd had my fingers burned.

John Clarke

Schoolbell Haiku

Why does the bell peal
laughter? It knows each teacher
was also a child.

Debjani Chatterjee

Netball

When
trying
to score
at netball
it helps
if you're
more
than
usually
normally
excess-
ively
extra-
ordinar-
ily
tall.

Ann Bonner

Some Days

Some days this school
is a huge concrete sandwich
squeezing me out like jam.

It weighs so much
breathing hurts, my legs freeze
my body is heavy.

On days like that
I carry whole buildings
high on my back.

Other days
the school is a rocket
thrusting right into the sun.

It's yellow and green
freshly painted,
the cabin windows
gleam with laughter.

On days like that
whole buildings support me,
my ladder is pushing
over their rooftops.

313

Amongst the clouds
I'd need a computer
to count all the bubbles
bursting aloud in my head.

David Harmer

I take me for granted

I take me for granted,
my cortex, my skin,
a membrane of mystery
that's holding me in.

My archway of eyebrows,
my tongue and my ears,
my speckles of freckles,
my colour, my tears.

My veins like a river,
my liver – a pearl,
my chromosomes name me
a boy or girl.

My heart, a silk engine –
both fragile and strong,
my chorus of blood cells,
a cherry red song.

My lungs, a ribbed grotto
as confirmed by X-ray,
unparalleled fortune
of my DNA.

I take me for granted.
What exactly's a gland?
Such things I don't know . . .
. . . like the back of my hand.

Stewart Henderson

The I-Spy Book of Teachers

One point if you catch your teacher yawning.
Double that to two if later on you find her snoring.
Three points if you hear your teacher singing
and four if it's a pop song not a hymn.
A generous five points if you ever see them jogging
and six if you should chance upon them snogging.

Seven if you ever find her on her knees and praying
for relief from noisy boys who trouble her.
Eight if you should catch him in the betting shop,
nine if you see him dancing on *Top of the Pops*.
And ten if you hear her say what a lovely class she's got
for then you'll know there's something
   quite seriously wrong with her.

Brian Moses

Mr Body, Our Head

Our Head, Mr Body, is six feet tall.
He's always on his toes and he has a heart of gold.
He has a finger in every pie
and a chip on his shoulder.

He doesn't stand for any cheek
and so we don't give him any lip
and we *never* talk back.

Mr Body knows when we're pulling his leg.
he says, 'Now just you hold your tongue.
I want you to knuckle under and toe the line.
I want no underhand tricks in my school!'

He says our new school
cost an arm and a leg to build.
He had to fight for it tooth and nail.

Mr Body says he shoulders the burden of responsibility
and ends up doing the work of four people.

That must make him a forehead.

John Rice

Mr Marks and the Seasons

It's autumn today.
The wind is blowing.
It's chilly.
I know that it's autumn because
Mr Marks is sweeping up the leaves.

It's winter today.
The sky is grey.
It's very cold.
I know that it's winter because
Mr Marks is putting salt on the yard.

It's spring today.
The air smells fresh.
The light is bright.
I know that it's spring because
Mr Marks is checking the tadpoles.

It's summer today.
The field's been cut.
We throw the grass about.
I know that it's summer because
Mr Marks is putting out the parasols.

Jill Dove

Nature Table

On the nature table
There's a conker
And a sticky twig

A pebble
A mermaid's purse
And a dead earwig

A fossil
Some nuts
And a shell from the shore

A bean, a bean
Another bean
And Billy's old apple core

Roger Stevens

The Harvest Queen
(or Corn Mother, who controls all the seasons)

Since sown
in spring
she's grown.
Sun has warmed
and rains
have fed her.
Winds have blown.

Crows have flown
above the fields now shorn
of ripened corn.
Drowsy poppies shown
their dazzling red.

319

Blackberries glisten.
Swallows gather
from the eaves.
The sheaves
of wheat collected.
The first leaves fall.

The golden corn
is Queen of all
the Harvest. The store
Is full. Winter is
provided for.

Ann Bonner

Harvest

Pumpkin and apple,
potato and plum.
What time of year
does harvest-time come?

Harvest's in autumn –
the time I like best.
Gold and ripe,
fruit-time, *harvest!*

Joan Poulson

320

School Photo
Haiku

Don't ask me to smile.
The gap in my teeth must not
be revealed. Lips sealed.

Ann Bonner

Help!

Dear Mrs Berry
As you are our head teacher
I thought you should know
That I'm writing you this letter
On the floor under my table
Where I have accidentally on purpose
Dropped my pencil
I need to let you know quite urgently
That our supply teacher, Mr Pigge

Has gone mad. He ranted and raved at us
Using a lot of shouting and spit
Then he stapled Kieron to the wall
And tied Nicola to the door by her plaits
Now he's looking at me.

Whoops! Nearly got caught then!
Fortunately, when he threw his chair at me
I was still under the table
Sadly it hit the five kids next to me
Sent them flying I can tell you!
I can also report that Lucy
Has been glued to the floor for whispering
And Daniel, Gurteak and Sam
Were dumped in the bins by the boiler house
Jade, Sally and Lackveer are crying
And Josh has been shoved head first
Into the gerbil cage.

Hello Mrs Berry
I'm writing this from the cupboard where
Ten of us have been locked away
For writing notes in class.
I think Mr Pigge is asleep now
I can probably sneak this note

Through a crack in the back
Hoping that you will find it very quickly.
Please rescue us before home time
Unless it's maths homework tonight, in which case
Please leave us here till Monday.

Your friend Jack
In Year Five

David Harmer

October

In Front of Me

They say it right in front of me
As if I wasn't there
They think
If I'm not looking
I can't hear:

I'm listening
Look closely – I'm aware.

JonArno Lawson

Squirrels and Motorbikes

Today we went out of school
Down the lane
Into the spinney
To watch squirrels

We saw lots of grey squirrels
Scuttling through the trees
Searching for nuts on the ground
Some as still as statues

We all took notes
Made sketches
And asked questions

Back in school
We drew our squirrels
Some sitting like
Silver grey coffee-pots
While others paddled acorns
Into the soft green grass
Some still listening with their tufty ears
Others with their feather-duster tails waving

Everyone drew a squirrel picture – except
George, who drew a motorbike
But then, he always does.

David Whitehead

In School

In school everyone has to be
Good at something.

I'm good at keeping quiet so
No one notices.

Lucinda Jacob

Shut Down

You watch your shoes step and scuff.
Your heavy school-bag swings around.
Worry-words rattle against your teeth.
You've seen enough and you've shut down.

You've lost your senses one by one;
a sleepwalker, barely feeling the ground.
Too many raised voices, slamming doors.
You've heard enough and you've shut down.

Above you, a cloud forms the shape of your face,
a twist of wind makes it frown.
A shaft of sunlight strokes your hair,
but you've felt enough and you've shut down.

'Look up here,' whispers the tree.
A single blackbird calls your name.
The promise of rain is sweet on your tongue.
But you've had enough and you've shut down.

Mandy Coe

The Imaginative Schoolchild

On my way to school
I saw an alligator.
He gave a toothy smile
and said he'd see me later.

Next I met a dragon
with shiny happy eyes.
He promised me a lollipop
as a nice surprise.

I walked a little further
and there I met a snake.
He told me a silly joke
and I gave him some cake.

The lady I bumped into next
wore a pointed hat.
She was polite enough to me
and let me stroke her bat.

And when I finally got to school
I met my classroom teacher,
he had five legs and insect eyes,
a most intriguing creature.

Angela Topping

Visiting Poet

Holding up the spoon
we were asked to write
'Just a list of words.'
What do you see when I hold this spoon?

At ease with my teacher's expertise,
I began to write.
I knew the score and didn't share
my charges' apprehension.

What do I see?
The spoon is unwashed,
a symbol of my dereliction.
Duty – stained and tarnished.
Thus have I measured my life.

While Joanne, tiny and almost mute
for three weeks now,
gazing at the spoon
saw the moon.

John Clarke

Good morning

this is
the teacher forecast

Mrs Brown
will be gloomy with occasional outbreaks of rage,
storms are expected by mid-afternoon

Miss Green
will be mild, although her smiles
will probably cloud over when she finds
the spider in her chalk box

Mr White
will be rather windy, especially after dinner-time,
with poor visibility when his glasses fog over

Some drizzle is expected around Miss Red,
she has not quite got over her cold,
and Mrs Blue is already gusting down the corridor
and should reach gale force 9 when she hits the
    playground.

For the rest of you, it will be much as usual,
a mixture of sunny moments and sudden heavy showers.
Have a good day.

Dave Calder

8

Out of Hours

When the footsteps fade,
when shadows deepen,
you can see the school
corridor as it is,
with its pale notices,
its returning gift
of echo returning,
the way it has
of suddenly leading
nowhere at all.

Lawrence Sail

Underneath the School

Just underneath the school there's often clay
And slugs and sand, and maybe Roman bones
A Celt or two as well, perhaps a Pict?
Who really knows what's underneath the school?

Dig deeper down through layers and layers of crust,
Down through the mantle's hidden veins of ore
Beyond, the heat's too awful to ignore –
Like you yourself, earth has a molten core.

JonArno Lawson

Mister Nobody

I'm a spook from the toilets
I'm the ghost without a name
a head without a body
it's really a crying shame.

I'm not on the ghoul register
I never get near a class,
the janitor just ignores me
won't even give me a visitor's pass –

No name you see!

I still do what a spirit does
I scream and screech and wail
blow my frosty misty breath
and scare spooked pupils pale –

With fright you see!

Keen to state my spectre's case
I've a meeting with the head
but I don't hold out too much hope
he'll remind me I'm already dead!

Perhaps *you* could help me out
any name you think of would do
then I'd be allowed to come to class

and sit

right here

right next

to you!

Brian Whittingham

The Playground

A ringing bell
A mass of noise
A surge of youth
A chanting rhyme
A shouting mouth
A flying ball
A bleeding knee
A runny nose
A taunting sneer
A pushing hand
A lonely face
A crying soul
A pestered man
A piercing call
A line of hope
An empty space

Marie Thom

Inside Sir's Matchbox

Our teacher's pet
Lives in a nest of pencil-shavings
Inside a matchbox
Which he keeps
In the top drawer of his desk.
It's so tiny, he says,
You need a microscope to see it.
When we asked him what it ate,
He grinned and said,
'Nail clippings and strands of human hair –
Especially children's.'
Once, on Open Day,
He put it out on the display table,
But we weren't allowed to open the box,
Because it's allergic to light.

Our teacher says his pet's unique.
'Isn't it lonely?' we asked.
'Not with you lot around,' he said.

Once, there was an awful commotion
When it escaped
While he was opening the box
To check if it was all right.
But he managed to catch it
Before it got off his desk.

Since then, he hasn't taken it out much.
He says he thinks it's hibernating at present –
Or it could be pregnant.
If it is, he says,
There'll be enough babies
For us all to have one.

John Foster

After School Club

I like Tuesdays.
Compared to the rest
Tuesdays are the best.

We study knights and castles
– but it's not history,
We look at birds and animals
– but it's not nature study,
We encounter kings and queens
– but nothing to do with monarchy,
We even meet a bishop
– but no other religious study,
We move forwards, backwards and diagonally
– yet it's not PE.

I like Tuesdays.
Compared to the rest
Tuesdays are the best
'Cause we play chess. Oh yes!

Ruth Underhill

When Ms Smith Slammed the Classroom Door

It frightened up a flock of pigeons on the back field.
It made the Yorkshire puddings
collapse with a sigh.

It didn't crack ceilings.
It didn't make wars.
It didn't make the summer holidays any shorter.

But it did play on our minds over and over
and over.

Mandy Coe

Science stinks

Science stinks

And that's not all.

It fizzes, flashes, bubbles, bangs,
Grows, glows, pulls, pushes,
Moves, murmurs, hums, growls,
Crawls, creeps, bleeds, breeds,

Tries, tests, bends, breaks,
Makes, mends, clones, cures,
Probes, peers, seeks, finds,
Clears, steers, leads, links.

Don't you love it?

Science stinks.

Paul Bright

After School

We wait all day
for after school
for the bell to go
for the chairs to be stacked
for the chalk dust to settle
when the teachers relax
for the pell mell
helter skelter
race for the gates
where the gangs all wait
to settle old scores
conker fights

and nosebleeds
and wild bully roars
then the games of chain-chase
till the sun starts to dip
turn to catch-the-girl
kiss-the-girl
quick as quick
winding home past the sweet shop
for penny chews
where the paper boys huddle
to take out the news
till dawdling back alleys
and grim fingered trees
lead us shadowing slowly
home for our teas

Dave Ward

The Bell

I am the bell.
I rule the school.

When I ring,
Classes snap to attention.

341

Anyone who ignores me
Risks a detention.

When I ring,
Latecomers start running.
Teachers put down their coffee cups
And sigh.
Playground games stop.
Children line up.

I am the bell.
I carve the day into chunks.
I summon everyone to assembly
And decide when it's time for dinner.

I'm in control
Everyone listens to me.
With my shrill voice
I can empty the playground
And the staffroom.

In an emergency,
I can clear the whole school
In less than three minutes.

I am the bell.
I rule the school.

John Foster

Words Behaving Badly

Words
Develop nasty habits –
Getting out of order,
Going off at tangents,
Breaking rules,
Attention seeking.
Give them fifty lines.
They take delight
In ambushing the reader,
Going round in gangs
With their unsuitable friends
Imagining they're poems!
Words –
I'd keep an eye on them
If I were you.

Sue Cowling

The Ascent of Vinicombe

He took his bag off his back and strapped it to his chest.
I think this is the start of an adventure, he declared, and
  so it was. With great care we roped ourselves together,
then slowly, cautiously, we fought our way up the ice-cliff.
He led, of course, shouting warnings and encouragement
  as he sprang
from boulder to boulder, dodging avalanches. It was hard
  going.
There was no shelter from the bitter wind and only one
lamp-post strong enough to bear our weight. We paused a
  moment
then pressed on, any delay was dangerous. Without
  warning
the pavement would split, opening horrid pits, crevasses
crammed with writhing snakes or hairy mammoths. Despite
  it all,
we struggled upwards, risking a traverse of the slippery
  railings,

until we hauled each other, wild-eyed and wind-beaten,
   across the glacier
of Kersland Street. It was then that, with amazing speed,
he slipped his coat off and hung it cape-like from his head,
announced his possession of super-powers and flew, arms
   outstretched,
up the lane towards the school.

Dave Calder

These are the Hands

These are the hands that wave
These are the hands that clap
These are the hands that pray
These are the hands that tap

These are the hands that grip
These are the hands that write
These are the hands that paint
These are the hands that fight

These are the hands that hug
These are the hands that squeeze
These are the hands that point
These are the hands that tease

These are the hands that fix
These are the hands that mend
These are the hands that give
These are the hands that lend

These are the hands that take
These are the hands that poke
These are the hands that heal
These are the hands that stroke

These are the hands that hold
These are the hands that love
These are the hands of mine
That fit me like a glove

Paul Cookson

Ms Spry

Sweet Miss Spry
Seems rather shy,
But Ben and I
Think she's a spy,
Living in a shady dive
And being paid by MI5.

John Kitching

Careers Advice

Johnson.
You're good at staring into space.
You can be an astronaut.

Patel.
You're good at copying other people's answers,
especially upside down.
You can be a magician.

Chivers.
You're good at making up excuses.
You can be a politician.

Diggory.
You're good at shouting.
You can sell fruit and vegetables.

Matthews.
You're good at truancy.
You can be the space
into which Johnson stares.

Steve Turner

The Ghosts of the Children Who Attended This School Before Us

Odd bumps, occasional thumps
will tell you they are still here –
hidden in the shadowy corners
of the school corridors and playground.

They appear like flares
or slender comets of laser light
blazing through the classroom each time
we turn out the lights after
a winter school-day.

And each Christmas,
when teachers and children
troop to church for the school concert,
their voices echo our prayers
and sing descant to our carols.

We know them
as well as we know
those who will attend
this school after us – our daughters, our sons.

John Rice

Where Teachers
Keep Their Pets

Mrs Cox has a fox
nesting in her curly locks.

Mr Spratt's tabby cat
sleeps beneath his bobble hat.

Miss Cahoots has various newts
swimming in her zip-up boots.

Mr Spry has Fred his fly
eating food stains from his tie.

Mrs Groat shows off her stoat
round the collar of her coat.

Mr Spare's got grizzly bears
hiding in his spacious flares.

And . . .

Mrs Vickers has a stick insect called 'Stickers'
. . . but no one's ever seen where she keeps it.

Paul Cookson

School Crime

'So you say your school's been burgled',
    the policeman scratched his face,
'And there's nothing left to write with . . .
    . . . this looks like a pencil case!'

John Rice

Teacher's Very Quiet Today

Teacher's very quiet today,
hasn't shouted once
but just let us get on with things
in a casual sort of way.

Several times I caught her gaze
but I wasn't even noticed.
Teacher looks preoccupied
like something's weighing heavy on her mind.

I don't know what it is
but I think I've seen that look before.
The expression seems familiar,
though not in school,

It's more like the look dad had
when he crashed his new car
or when mum found out
that Auntie Jo was ill.

Teacher's very quiet today,
hasn't shouted once
but just let us get on with things
in a casual sort of way.

Paul Cookson

27

School For Wizards and Witches

> 2nd Witch: *Fillet of a fenny snake*
> *In the cauldron boil and bake.*
> William Shakespeare *Macbeth*, Act 4 Sc.1

So today, children, we will learn to make
   Fillet of a fenny snake.
Now now, Caspar, none of your moans and groans;
   Get on with it and remove those bones.

No, Mervyn, not a *funny* snake. Fenny!
   It comes from a fen, Kenny.
That's lovely, really disgusting, Matilda.
   No dear. I don't know what killed her.

Matilda, show the others your fillet.
      No, Simon. We can't grill it.
It's for our spell. Caspar, for badness' sake
      Give Sybil back her fenny snake.

Give it back, child. You've got one of your own.
      And leave those poisoned entrails alone.
No, Sybil. Slice lengthwise; by candlelight.
      Get Merle to show you. Yes, that's right.

Lobo. Take that poisonous toad off your shoulder.
      Put it in your coursework folder.
I've told you ninety-nine times. You know the rule:
      No pets. No pets allowed in school.

Careful, Nostrodamus, don't spill that slime!
      Where's my hourglass? Is that the time!?
Everything away! Whooshky-cadabra! That's right!
      Or we won't be home before midnight.

You've all been really evil today.
      So tomorrow I'll give you an hour's play
While I bake the snake. But look at that sky!
      Badnight, wizlets. I must fly.

Gerard Benson

Hello, Mr Visitor

Hello, Mr Visitor
Have you come to visit Miss?
Are you her boyfriend?
D'you want to give her a kiss?

Are you a parent
Who's come up to complain?
Or are you the plumber
Who's come to fix the drain?

Are you an inspector
Who's come to test our skill?
Is that why the headteacher
Is looking pale and ill?

Are you the dreaded ghost
Of the teacher who said:
'You'll be the death of me!'
And dropped down dead?

Hello, Mr Visitor
Who would you like to see?
Welcome to our school
Whoever you may be!

John Foster

It's True

I don't believe yer.
It's true, a big hairy one.

Geroff, you'd hear it.
Some have, screeching at night.

But what does he feed it?
The lines of those kept in at break.

No bird would eat those.
Who said it was a bird?

You did.
No, I never. There's other things

than birds go screeching at night.
It makes its nest in chalk dust.

Now I know you're fibbing.
I'm not, actually.

OK, then, why has no one ever seen it?
Some have, shifting from foot

to foot in the stock cupboard.
Have you?

No. *But I dare you to go.*
No way. I don't care what

sort of animal that is, there's no way
I'd try and look in that stock cupboard.

You know what sir's like.
We'd better get these lines done

before the bell goes.
I must not witter on in class.
I must not witter on in class.
I must not witter on i

Angela Topping

Net Ball

Beyond harvest, autumn half term,
the moon round and solid.
The car swings round the Suffolk lanes,

Mum grips the wheel, a quick turn,
hand over hand, then a swivel back.

She seems to know the tricks

of the game, passing the moon from
one side of the road to the other.
Each time it bounces back, till

on a straight stretch, it is caught
for a moment in a net of branches.
Brilliant shot, Mum.

Liz Cashdan

Timetable

First-year ghosts, 9 p.m.,
First class, 'Elementary Moaning',
10 p.m. at local churchyard,
'Get to Grips with Graveyard Groaning',
10.30, practical,
'How to Remove your Head',
12 midnight, back to churchyard,
'Seven Steps to Wake the Dead',
1 a.m., 'Dragging Chains',
2 a.m., 'Ringing Bells',
3 a.m., 'To Mix Fake Blood',
4 a.m., 'Revolting Smells',
5 a.m., dawn instruction,
'Murky Mists and Spooky Lighting',
5.30, theory class,
'The Basics of Successful Frightening',
6 a.m., lost property,
Please reclaim your missing head,
6.30, class dismissed,
Vanish, fade or float to bed.

Julia Rawlinson

November

L is for Library

Don't be fooled!

A library may LOOK like a room,
But really, it is a magical street
Lined with many-coloured doors.

Walk through this one,
And step back, back,
To far-away places
Where Romans march, or castles glitter,
Or small children skate
On a frozen river.

Open this one,
And enter the dark cage of a jungle
Where great, black cats watch you
With golden eyes,
And emerald insects flit around your head
Like living jewels.

Try this one,
And massive machines will roar
And spit fire at you like story monsters,
While excited inventors amaze you
With their electronic tricks.

Or what about this door?
The one with the dragon-head handle?
Let it creak wide and welcome you
To endless Wonderlands.
Here are white rabbits, of course.
And sorrowful, grey donkeys,
And wizards, and wild woods,
And stormy seas,
And stolen treasures,
And purple planets,
And talking mice,
And all the beasts that ever were,
Or NEVER were –
The unicorn, the phoenix,
And your very own, flying horse.

Gallop away!
Explore all the doors,
Discover the wide world that is called
Imagination,
And you will not be fooled
By clever disguises.

A library only LOOKS like a room.

Clare Bevan

Schooldays

In school I feel
like a salmon swimming upstream
a hibernating bear too slow
to hunt. A three-legged fox, still
dragging the phantom trap around.

The teachers are heat-seeking missiles,
the pupils, a pesky swarm
of bloodthirsty bugs.
And despite the crowded rooms and corridors
I am always alone.

Linda Lee Welch

Bullies

With the eye in the back of his head
he sees them coming –

eight-year-old breakers,
baby-hard, baby-soft.

Their space-machine, so elegant
could swallow him,

drown him once and for all
in a dish of air.

No use trying to rewrite the law:
they are the masters –

skills bred in the bone.
He freezes –

they expect it,
though a voice inside him squeaks

I . . . Words cut his tongue,
weigh in his mind like a bruise.

Katherine Gallagher

Looking Forward to Divali

Divali light
will cheer the dark
November night.

We decorate
the classroom wall
to celebrate.

Each Hindu
hears Rama's tale
and knows it's true.

Be joyful then.
Our festival
is here again.

Ann Bonner

The School Fireworks Show

Squelch of boots and torchlight from cars then . . .

woomph . . . crackle, crackle, blooming blue, ooh,
woomph . . . crackle, crackle, yellow willow, oh,
woomph . . . crackle, crackle, crimson necklace, wow,
   thistledown whistling, aah,
woomph . . . crackle, crackle, green glister, wheee, spilt
   bags of sherbet, limelight, aah . . .

pop, pop, pop . . . waving ferns of silver, weaving like silk
   worms,
pop, pop, pop . . . geysers of tinsel, Titanic red wishes,
   swishes of harmless alarm,
pop, pop, pop . . . gushes of amber, rambling Ss, a
   meandering span to
pop, pop, pop . . . gashes of green flushing the darkness,
   brushing it clean with mint . . .

poomph . . . fizzle, chizzle, screaming shooters, wheels
   coming off,
poomph . . . swizzle, twizzle, streamers unrolling, sizzling
   at the ends,
poomph . . . frizzle, whizzle, frying pan spitting with
   hatching asps,

poomph . . . spizzle, drizzle, silver quick-splitting into
  millions of specks . . .

whoosh, pepperpot climbing . . . boom, diamond dust
  hanging . . . then black,
whoosh, pepperpot climbing . . . boom, emeralds
  spreading . . . then black,
whoosh, pepperpot climbing . . . boom, armfuls of
  amethyst . . . then black,
whoosh, pepperpot climbing . . . boom, rash of rubies . . .
  then black . . .

pop, popping up . . . bagatelle of baubles bouncing off
  pins,
pop, popping up . . . a gale heaving with autumn leaves,
pop, popping up . . . tail lights snaking up hairpins,
pop, popping up . . . a sluice of sequins unleashed . . .

whoosh, saltbox climbing . . . boom, Neptune's net
  spreading . . . then black,
whoosh, saltbox climbing . . . boom, gold rush through
  space . . . then black,
whoosh, saltbox climbing . . . boom, zapping past
  planets . . . then black,
whoosh, saltbox climbing . . . boom, zooming to a chrome
  infinity . . . then black . . .

pop, pop, pop . . . frilly foreground of frothing
   phosphorus, aah,
woomph . . . crackle, crackle, halos dilating, cymbal
   crescendo, oh,
pop, popping up . . . bangles of rainbow, intoxicating
   cocktails mixing, gee,
poomph, sawtooth splinters . . . screeching flea bites,
   slipping drill bits, ooh,
whoosh, pepperpots climbing . . . bang-studded skies, star-
   studded eyes, aah . . .

then torchlight and squelch of boot to cars
and oohs and aahs all the way home . . . .

Paddy Hughes

6

Bird

Sometimes being your best friend
Makes me feel like a little bird
With my beak stretched open
Ruffling my feathers,
Hungry.

Lucinda Jacob

Poems Don't Have to Rhyme

Miss Moss says poems
Don't have to rhyme
But they do have to skip
And weave and dip
And wheel and flip
And zoom and zip
Like an oojah-ma-flip
And stumble and trip
Or float like a ship
Or a boat on the lip
Of a wave or let rip
Or be cool and be hip
Or lie down for a kip
Poems have to have a good time
But poems don't have to rhyme

Roger Stevens

What Mr Kenning Does When He Thinks We Aren't Looking

Space gazer
Nostril wrinkler
Idle doodler
Paper crinkler

Tie fiddler
Fly checker
Blue-tac moulder
Paper clip wrecker

Pen-top sucker
Teeth grinder
Fingernail nibbler
Watch winder

Rubber sniffer
Pencil roller
Song hummer
Ipod scroller

Burp stifler
Eye closer
Paper reader
Nearly dozer

Ear-hole cleaner
Fluff flicker
Toffee chewer
Nose picker

Paul Cookson

Lunchtime

There's a sandwich in my lunchbox.
Just what I like,
Cheese and cucumber.
Yum!

Then my best friend says
That's a stupid sandwich!
Stupid sandwich! Stupid sandwich!

Now I don't like my sandwich any more.

Lucinda Jacob

Wants and Needs

I want a Science lesson
that lists the seven seas
that names the seven continents
explains what lightning means
and thunder, and the smell of rain
the miracle of birth
the Seven Wonders of the World
the grace of planet Earth.

I need a Science lesson
that will tell me what to do
about melting icecaps, sulphur rain,
energy we can't renew.
Species face extinction,
sea water's on the rise.
I need to take some action
before we're out of time.

Linda Lee Welch

The School Bag

It's in my bag, sir!

Jerking the zip
Taking a look
Hand stretching in
Found text book

Just a minute, sir!

Delving deeper
Pens and tissue
Wad of paper
One sports shoe

I've nearly got it, sir!

Digits grabbing
Protractor chipped
Half-noshed apple
School tie snipped

It's here somewhere, sir!

Another rummage
Conker cracked
Aged acorn
Peanut snack

Honestly, sir!

The backpack's limp
Sides depleted
Few crumbs and fluff
Search completed

No homework.
Again.
See me after class!

Ruth Underhill

School

Footsteps walking
Teachers talking
Parents parking
Registers marking
Late ones dashing
Water splashing
Glue pots sticking
Clock hands ticking
Children chatting
Paintdrops splatting
Hard chairs scraping
Dropped clothes draping
Pages turning
Keen minds learning
Cutlery clattering
Custard splattering
Clean plates stacking
Ladies yacking
Trainers dancing
Weigh scales balancing
Music drifting
Scientists sifting
Keyboards tapping

Small hands clapping
Wood tools sawing
Pencils drawing
Trowels digging
Best friends tigging
Soft balls throwing
Needles sewing
Voices singing
Loud bell ringing
Footsteps flying
Teachers sighing

SILENCE.

Marie Thom

Their Secret Is Out!

Teachers are not normal.
Anybody knows that –
Only they pretend to be like us
By shopping in the supermarket
And buying jam and cornflakes.
It's a con.
They don't eat.

They are not real inside their bodies –
They are full of wires and micro-circuits.
They feed on mathematics
And spellings like *psoriasis* and *bouillabaisse*.
Do not believe them when they tell you they were young
   once.
It is a lie.
The factory that makes them
Does not do 'young'.
It only makes three sorts:
Bat-eared,
Needle-nosed,
And Eagle-eyed.

Jan Dean

Misleading Reading

Miss caught me scribbling on the desk
So I, while smiling sweetly,
Replied: 'I am not *scribbling*, Miss –
You'll find I'm writing NEATLY!'

Graham Denton

Out of Class

It was that last half hour in the morning –
Coming up to dinner time and I was trying
To finish my 'five sentences about myself'

And I couldn't remember how many Rs in 'embarrassed'
And when Miss Lyon sent me to the Secretary
With the Games List I was quite pleased because

You can duck into the Library and ask Mrs Hofmann.
Although she's German she can spell any English word
Better than anybody. Year four were watching telly in
    Resources

And there was a boy standing outside Mr Devon's room,
Like always. Sometimes there are two, one each side
Of the door. He won't let them stand together.

When I went through the Lower Hall the ladies
Were putting the tables out and joking to each other
And one of them dropped a tray full of knives and forks

With a crash and said something not very ladylike.
I pretended not to hear. The piano was open and someone
Had drawn a cartoon face on the board; and year three

Had left the recorders all anyhow on the stage blocks.
I knocked on the Office door and the new Secretary
With the bright red nails just took the list off me

Without looking at me. There was that smell of stew.
I heard Mrs Foyl shouting so I went back via the toilets.
As soon as I picked up my pen I realized I'd forgotten

To ask Mrs Hofmann, so I guessed and put in two Rs
And that turned out to be right (Exclamation Mark!)
But I missed out one of the Ss. Just my luck.

Then Miss Docherty next door must have let hers out early
Because you could hear them all squealing in the corridor.
And then little Simon Orimbo came round ringing the bell.

Gerard Benson

16

Writing

Sometimes
Words come
Into my head
In patterns.

Sometimes
They even
Mean something.

Lucinda Jacob

17

Cobweb Morning

On a Monday morning
We do spellings and Maths.
And silent reading.

But on Monday
After the frost
We went straight outside.

Cobwebs hung in the cold air,
Everywhere.
All around the playground,
They clothed the trees,
Dressed every bush
in veils of fine white lace.

Each web,
A wheel of patient spinning.
Each spider,
Hidden,
Waiting.

Inside,
We worked all morning
To capture the outside.

Now
In our patterns and poems
We remember
The cobweb morning.

June Crebbin

St Judas Welcomes Author Philip Arder

Welcome to St Judas.
Because of a mix-up in timetabling
Miss Horace who was supposed to be looking after you
    today
has had to go on a factory field-trip
with gifted and talented and the two classes
of students who've actually read your book.
We've had to put you with a younger group
who, like me I must confess, have never heard of you,
but we did look you up on Wikipedia
and see that you like cats.

Perhaps you could tell a story with lots of actions
and they could pretend to be their favourite animals?

There's a note here from Miss H saying that
we are unable to buy any of your books for the library
because we've spent the budget for this school term.
The children won't be able
to purchase any of your books either,
following a change of rules recently agreed by the PTA.
We have arranged, however, for you to sign
lots of scraps of paper
of ever-diminishing
sizes.

And for you to give two extra talks,
seeing as how you're here.

A photographer from the local paper
has a small window in his busy schedule
so can only come halfway through your first event.
At this stage, we will have to stop proceedings
and remove from shot those children whose parents
have not given consent for them to be photographed.
It shouldn't take long.

And I should warn you that
there are certain children
unsuitable for audience participation.
We found that out the hard way.

I'm going to have to leave you here
in the staff room for a while
while I find an alternative venue.
Mock exams in the main hall
mean that you'll probably have to give your
little talks in the dining room.
I'll ask the kitchen staff to keep the noise
of table-laying
to a minimum.

I'm afraid I'll have to nip out part way through
your first event
to sort out a health and safety issue
but Mrs Lomax will be there throughout,

though she does have to finish
a pile of marking.
Mr Goody, our PE teacher, will be just down the corridor
and has promised to keep an ear out for the kids
if they get restless.
At that age, they're easily bored.

I'm sorry if things seem a little disorganized
but you must be used to it.
I imagine the big names don't do school visits,
do they?
Have you ever met Philip Pullman,
by the way?
His books are amazing.

Ah, there goes the bell.

Help yourself to coffee.
The mugs are in the sink . . .

Philip Ardagh

Schooldays End

When I was built, children walked
for miles, called by my iron bell.
No cars, electric light or felt-pens.
Just hurrying feet, the hiss of gas
and the squeal of chalk on slate.

They say that I am haunted now.
My attic creaks, twisted black gates
bang in the wind. A shadow-game
flickers across the yard. Now, the children
hurry past me to the new school. I see them

carrying their toys and picture-books,
their lunch-boxes and football boots.
The new school is warm and full of music,
its windows bright with cutout shapes.
Mine are dark and broken.

This long night is the last.
Moonlight spills down my slate roof.
I wish my bell could ring out again:
Come to me children! Run! Run!
Tomorrow the bulldozers come.

Mandy Coe

Where Do Ideas Come From?

I once found an idea for a poem
Down the back of the sofa.
It was just out of reach,
Which was annoying,
And I had to reach down
Behind the cushions,
Right up to my elbow,
To fetch it out.

I also found a pound coin.

Roger Stevens

Easy Does It

I'm enjoying a classroom daydream
while you all do a test.
I look as though I'm working hard
but I'm really having a rest.

I appear to be keeping an eye on you
but it's not you I see.
I'm imagining a sunny beach.
Picturing a deep blue sea.

Without lifting a finger
I've got you under my thumb.
For once *I'm* taking it easy.
I'm actually having fun!

I look as though I'm working hard
but I'm really having a rest.
I'm enjoying a classroom daydream.
You're struggling with a test.

Bernard Young

A Proper Poet

Today we have a real-live poet in school –
This gentleman who's standing next to me.
I must say when I met him in the entrance,
He was not as I imagined he would be.

I'd always thought that poets were tall and wan,
With eyes as dark and deep as any sea,
So when I saw this jolly little man,
He didn't seem a proper poet to me.

The poets I've seen in pictures dress in black
With velvet britches buttoned at the knee,
So when I saw the T-shirt and the jeans,
He didn't look a proper poet to me.

I've read that famous poets are often ill,
And die consumptive deaths on a settee.
Well I'd never seen a healthier-looking man
He just didn't look a proper poet to me.

My favourite poems are by Tennyson and Keats.
This modern stuff is not my cup of tea,
So when I heard our poet was keen on rap
He didn't sound a proper poet to me.

Well, I'm certain that we'll all enjoy his poems
And listen – after all, we've paid his fee –
I hope that they're in verses and they rhyme
For that is proper poetry – to me.

Gervase Phinn

The Head's First Name

It just slipped past his young wife's lips
as she stood – in a yellow dress
– calling and waggling her fingers
over the roof of her car.
And suddenly

we saw him
not as Sir,
with his dark suit and shiny briefcase.
Not as Mr stand-to-attention McGregor,
but as Frederick,
Fred,
Freddie.

And without taking his eyes off his shoes
he elbowed through
fifty hand-over-mouth grins,
the tips of his ears
glowing red.

Mandy Coe

Batgirl's Disgrace

Auntie Betty pulls her cloak on
And the mask – the one with ears
Then she flies out of the classroom
Fighting back a flood of tears
All the teachers in the playground
Wag their fingers at the girl
If only she had done her homework
FIRST, before she saved the world

Need calamity prevention?
Sorry, Batgirl's in detention.

Andrea Shavick

Painting

Yellow is my favourite colour;
I'm painting like the sun,
Yellow birds in golden bushes
Till all the yellow's done.

Green is my favourite colour;
I'm painting like the grass,
Green woods and fields and rushes,
The river flowing past.

Blue is my favourite colour;
I'm painting like the sea,
Blue sailing ships and fishes,
And icebergs floating free.

Red is my favourite colour;
I'm painting like a fire,
Red twigs, then blazing branches
As the flames leap higher.

Irene Rawnsley

What Does Poetry Do?

It nosedives from the top of the fridge
into a bowl of rapids,

it crawls along the floor
and taps you on the knee,

it changes the colour of a room,

it puts great wheezing slices of life
into bun trays, with or without punctuation.

It manages this all by itself.

Chrissie Gittins

School Survival Kit

Pack the following every day:

1. Friendship
   (Friends make everything great)

2. A big smile
   (Who can resist that?)

3. A head full of jokes
   (To make others laugh)

4. A dollop of curiosity
   (To keep lessons interesting)

5. A packet of daydreams
   (For when they're not)

6. An ounce of courage
   (To face your fears)

7. A full battery of energy
   (To make playtimes fun)

8. A taste for adventure
   (To enjoy school trips)

9. A little understanding
   (So you can forgive those who let you down)

10. A bag full of joy
    (To share)

Karen Costello-McFeat

The Last Laugh

Jacko floated over the corner
less than a minute, the score two-all
in our under-elevens cup-final.
I leapt like a salmon up a waterfall
high above the defence, meeting
the ball with a perfect header until
an elbow sharp as a bayonet
stuck into my side and cut out my breath.
I fell to the grass like a burst balloon
face down in the mud, the air knocked from me.
The ball, a useless, harmless bubble,
floated past the post towards the corner.
Their full-back's face, like a monster mask,
grinned as I slipped and slurped in the dirt.
He held out his arm to help me get up

then pushed me back over, whispering,
Got you that time, didn't I, mate,
thought you'd won? That'll teach you!
He straightened up, laughed again
when he heard the whistle he knew was full time.
But I saw the ref standing just behind him.
That whistle meant I was going to score
the match-winning goal from the penalty spot.

David Harmer

Playground Song

I'm the one in calipers
Who makes the people stare –
I used to lie awake at night
And think it wasn't fair,
But since I've found a proper friend
I really couldn't care . . .

She told her mum
                that I'm the one
With lovely curly hair.

Clare Bevan

The Interesting Table

There's a table which stands at the end of the class
With interesting things galore
If it's weird or curious
That's where it goes
It's what 'Interesting Tables' are for.

There's an adder's skin, mandolin, thingummyjig
From whatshisname's big sister's house;
A ball signed by Wigan Athletic
And a nit comb with one half-squashed louse.

When we bring something in we discuss it
Then write a poem or two
Miss Bell says it helps to imagine
What interesting objects might feel, say or do.

One day Justin Smethwick turned up with a bag
And a mischievous smile on his face
Then up to the table he boldly went
Put his interesting thing pride of place.

It was . . .

A TOMATO

'Really interesting, Justin!' the class all jeered
Miss Bell's bottom lip hit the floor
And she ushered him out of the classroom
To the interesting corridor.

Lindsay MacRae

December

Cold Day – Edinburgh

Before my eyes open,
I smell the crisp, clean, cold air.

Windows splashed with ferns of frost.
Too cold to wash,
Just straight into clothes,
Then downstairs to big bowls of porridge.

In the street the roofs and cars and trees
Are sugar-coated.
We stand and stamp our feet
As steaming kettles pour over
Frozen locks and windscreens.
Exhaust clouds boil
And mingle with the smell of the brewery.

We are driven slowly to school.

Grim-faced salt-wielding janitors
Destroy lethal slides
As we sit huddled over Bunsen burners in the lab.
Then the note from the Office arrives –
'The boiler can't take it,
The school is too cold.'

So we go home to frozen pipes
And hot chocolate,
To wrap up in travelling rugs,
Sit on the storage heater,
And watch *South Pacific* on the telly.

Colin McEwan

Thanks

Danke, merci, gracias
for the heat of the sun,
the kindness of teaching,
the smell of fresh bread.

Diolch, nkosi, shur-nur-ah-gah-lem
for the sound of sand,
children singing,
the book and the pen.

Dhannyabad, blagodaria, hvala
for the blue of small flowers,
the bobbing seal's head,
the taste of clean water.

Shukran gazillan, yakoke, nandi
for the stripe of the zebra,
the song of the chaffinch,
the gentleness of snails.

Mh goi, abarka, dhanyavaad
for the length of time,
the loveliness of eyelashes,
the arc of the ball.

Dziekuje, bhala hove, shakkran
for the excitement of falling,
the stillness of night,
my heart beating.

Mandy Coe

Hi Ho, Hi Ho

The teachers are digging a tunnel,
They're digging it deeper each day,
They dig it when we're in assembly,
And when we've been sent out to play.

They're using bent spoons from the Staff Room,
And coffee mugs ancient and stained,
They crawl into lessons exhausted
(And muddy as well, if it rains).

The roof is supported by rulers
And chair legs that splinter and swell,
The rubble is smuggled in handbags
And pockets and gym shoes as well.

The entrance is under the Stock Room,
It's hidden where nobody looks,
Disguised by a heap of lost jumpers,
And paper and dusty old books.

The teachers are filthy and frazzled,
Their bones are beginning to creak –
And NOBODY seems to have told them
We break up for Christmas next week!

Clare Bevan

Reading Round the Class

On Friday we have reading round the class.
Kimberley Bloomer is the best.
She sails slowly along the page like a great galleon
And everyone looks up and listens.
'Beautiful reading, Kimberley, dear,' sighs Mrs Scott,
'And with such fluency, such feeling.
It's a delight to hear.'

On Friday we have reading round the class.
I'm the worst.
I stumble and mumble along slowly like a broken-down
     train
And everyone looks up and listens.
Then they smile and snigger and whisper behind their
     hands.
'Dear me,' sighs Mrs Scott, 'rather rusty, Simon.
Quite a bit of practice needed, don't you think?
Too much television and football, that's your trouble,
And not enough reading.'

And she wonders why I don't like books.

Gervase Phinn

Early Winter Diary Poem

Six thirty;
    winter dawn –

scraping a thin skin
    of frost
from the windscreen –
    numb fingers fumble –
even the spray
    freezes.
The breeze is
    bitter –
It's so cold
    that stones crack –
that wool freezes
    on the sheep's back.

The birds are too still –
    even the sun
turns its back
    on the day;
but lazy wood-smoke
    idles
over Minchin's roof.

Pie Corbett

The Collector

Not for me woolly dolls
or football cards
pop star posters
model cars –
No, I'm into collecting adjectives . . .
  Big, fat, juicy, yummy, scrummy,
  rich and famous
  lean and keen
  kind of words.

I store them up for special occasions
  in – massive, marvellous,
    mysterious, magnificent
    adjectival boxes
  with secret seals
  and silver keys.

But, at the first stroke of the new millennium
my brother's bedside collection of !!!! marks
exploded with excitement
taking with them
the roof of our house
and
my superb adjective collection.

Request
    If you should ever find an adjective
    it is probably mine.
You know the sort of word I mean
    Lonely (cloud)
    misty (lace)
    sprightly (dance)
    pretty (place)
So if you ever see one
I'm sure it will be mine
unless it isn't spelt right
    – or doesn't seem to rhyme.

Peter Dixon

Mrs Smellie

Mrs Smellie
is a bit
of a
misnomer.
She's a perfume
fanatic
who loves
the aroma

of lavender
one day,
violets
another,
but we really
wouldn't
want any
other.
She's tulips
in spring,
she's summer
come early,
an oasis
of calm
in the hurly-
burly,
in the rough
and tumble
of life
at our school,
Mrs Smellie
is unbelievably
cool.

Brian Moses

Mr Walton's on the Playground

Michael's ball is on the roof
And Darren's looking for a fight
Little Kelly Cupcake
is dangling from her kite

But Mr Walton's on the playground
So everything will be all right

Noel went in the girls' loo
And gave the girls a fright
Yaseen won't let Gemma kiss him
But Derek Trubsall might

But Mr Walton's on the playground
So everything will be all right

Randeep's lost his pet rat
(He says it doesn't bite)
Michael says – Aren't people small
When viewed from this great height?

But Mr Walton's on the playground
So everything will be all right

Tommy's foot is swelling up
His laces are too tight
Now Michael's stuck up on the roof
He'll have to stay all night

But Mr Walton's on the playground
So everything will be er . . .

Where's Mr Walton gone?

Roger Stevens

Miss Creedle Teaches Creative Writing

'This morning,' cries Miss Creedle,
'We're all going to use our imaginations,
We're going to close our eyes 3W and imagine.
Are we ready to imagine, Darren?
I'm going to count to three.
At one, we wipe our brains completely clean;
At two, we close our eyes;
And at three, we imagine.
Are we all imagining? Good.
Here is a piece of music by Beethoven to help us.
Beethoven's dates were 1770 to 1827.

(See The Age of Revolutions in your History books.)
Although Beethoven was deaf and a German
He wrote many wonderful symphonies,
But this was a long time before anyone of us was born.
Are you imagining a time before you were born?
What does it look like? Is it dark?
(Embryo is a good word you might use.)
Does the music carry you away like a river?
What is the name of the river? Can you smell it?
Foetid is an exciting adjective.
As you float down the river
Perhaps you land on an alien planet.
Tell me what sounds you hear.
If there are indescribable monsters
Tell me what they look like but not now.
(Your book entitled *Tackle Pre-History This Way*
Will be of assistance here.)
Perhaps you are cast adrift in a broken barrel
In stormy shark-infested waters
(Remember the work we did on piranhas for RE?)
Try to see yourself. Can you do that?
See yourself at the bottom of a pothole in the Andes
With both legs broken
And your life ebbing away inexorably.
What does the limestone feel like?
See the colours.
Have you done that? Good.

And now you may open your eyes.
Your imagining time is over,
Now it is writing time.
Are we ready to write? Good.
Then write away.
Wayne, you're getting some exciting ideas down.
Tracy, that's lovely.
Darren, you haven't written anything.
Couldn't you put the date?
You can't think of anything to write.
Well, what did you see when you closed your eyes?
But you must have seen something beside the black.
Yes, apart from the little squiggles.
Just the black. I see.
Well, try to think
Of as many words for black as you can.'

Miss Creedle whirls about the class
Like a benign typhoon
Spinning from one quailing homestead to another.
I dream of peaceful ancient days
In Mr Swindell's class
When the hours passed like a dream
Filled with order and measuring and tests.

Excitement is not one of the things I come to school
    for.
I force my eyes shut

But all I see
Is a boy of twelve
Sitting at a desk one dark November day
Writing this poem.
And Darren is happy to discover
There is only one word for black
And that will have to suffice
Until the bell rings for all of us.

Gareth Owen

Teachers!

Teachers! I don't understand them.

They say:
   When you hand in your work,
   Make sure it's neat and tidy.
Then they mess it up
By scribbling illegible comments
All over it in red ink.

They say:
   Don't interrupt when I'm talking.
   Put your hand up
   And wait until I've finished.

But if they've got something to say,
They clap their hands
And stop your discussions in mid-sentence.

They say:
    Always plan your writing.
    Take your time. Think it through
    And do a rough draft.
Then they sit you in an examination hall
And ask you to write an essay
On one of six topics –
None of which interests you –
In an hour and a quarter.

They say:
    All work and no play
    Makes Jill a dull girl.
    Make sure you allow yourself
    Time off from your studies
    To relax and enjoy yourself.
Then, when you don't hand
Your homework in on time,
Because you took their advice,
They keep you in at lunch-time.

Teachers!
I don't understand them.

John Foster

Just Doing My Job

I'm one of Herod's Henchmen.
We don't have much to say,
We just charge through the audience
In a Henchman sort of way.

We all wear woolly helmets
To hide our hair and ears,
And wellingtons sprayed silver
To match our tinfoil spears.

Our swords are made of cardboard
So blood will not be spilled
If we trip and stab a parent
When the hall's completely filled.

We don't look VERY scary,
We're mostly small and shy,
And some of us wear glasses,
But we give the thing a try.

We whisper Henchman noises
While Herod hunts for strangers,
And then we all charge out again
Like nervous Power Rangers.

Yet when the play is over
And Miss is out of breath
We'll charge like Henchmen through the hall
And scare our Mums to death.

Clare Bevan

The Super Sledging Stars

A hard, hard winter. Snow lay deep and soft.
Sledges appeared from cellar, shed and loft.
We duffled-up from head to booted feet
And, with all the traffic stilled, reclaimed our street.
We made a slide that glinted like a gun,
and sledged non-stop on our own Cresta Run.

Lying, sitting, we rattled down the slope
then dragged our sledges back on reins of rope
until we reached the top. Then off we'd go
speed-bumping down the track of hard-packed snow.
Some fell, some squealed; the hopeless ones got miffed
when they got head-stuck in a roadside drift.

All day we sledge-raced down that icy slide.
At dusk the younger ones were called inside,
but we stayed on beneath the street lights' beam
and now our slide took on a silver gleam.
Fresh snowflakes fell, enshrouding roadside cars,
as we trudged home, the super sledging stars.

Wes Magee

Christmas Is Coming

Christmas is coming,
  The geese are getting fat,
Please to put a penny
  In the old man's hat.
If you haven't got a penny,
  A ha'penny will do;
If you haven't got a ha'penny,
  Then God bless you!

Anon.

Christmas Spirit

Friends
Friends
Friends
Friends
Friends
Friends
Friends
Friends
Friends
Friends
Friends
Friends
Friends

Katherine Gallagher

The Snowman

Once there was a snowman
Stood outside the door
Thought he'd like to come inside
And run around the floor;
Thought he'd like to warm himself
By the firelight red;
Thought he'd like to climb up
On that big white bed.
So he called the North Wind, 'Help me now, I pray.
I'm completely frozen, standing here all day.'
So the North Wind came along and blew him in the door,
And now there's nothing left of him
But a puddle on the floor!

Anon.

Christmas Music

Ten notes of music,
like snowflakes, drift and climb.

One rests on the wing of an angel
and that leaves nine.

Nine notes of music
sparkle bright and late.

One becomes the Christmas Star
and that leaves eight.

Eight notes of music,
carols sung in Devon.

One glides away on a moonbeam
and that leaves seven.

Seven notes of music,
curved as holly sticks.

One makes a shelter for a robin
and that leaves six.

Six notes of music
soar and twirl and dive.

One nestles in Mother Earth's arms
and that leaves five.

Five notes of music
chant old solstice lore.

One gets lost in the mountains
and that leaves four.

Four notes of music,
crystals on a tree.

One is melted by winter sun
and that leaves three.

Three notes of music:
crimson, silver, blue.

One rests on top of a fir tree
and that leaves two.

Two notes of music
children call in fun.

One whistled off by a snowman
and that leaves one.

One note of music
through all space and time

links us in love
at Winter's festival . . .
            Christmas song and rhyme.

Joan Poulson

After the End-of-Year Play

The janitor stands silently in the corner
As all the kids sing
And run
And cheer.
He watches as they all leave
Spring in their step
Excitedly talking
About Christmas.

Silently he turns out the lights
Of the empty classroom
Locking the door behind him.

He walks down the stairs,
Trudging towards the car park.

Silently he starts the car
And drives slowly through the snow,
To get home
And wait for next term.

Violet Macdonald

Remembering Snow

I did not sleep last night.
The falling snow was beautiful and white.
I went downstairs,
And opened the door.
I had not seen such snow before.
Our grubby little street had gone –
All things looked brand-new, and everywhere
There was a pureness in the air.
I felt such peace. Watching every flake
I felt more and more awake.
I thought I'd learned all there was to know
About the trillion million different kinds
Of swirling frosty flakes of snow.

420

But that was not so.
I did not know how vividly it lit
The world with such a peaceful glow.
Upstairs my parents slept.
I could not drag myself away from that sight
To call them down and have them share
The mute miracle of the snow.
It seemed to fall for me alone.
How beautiful our little street had grown!

Brian Patten

Coronation

Bring him a garland of bright winter jasmine,
Twine a gold chaplet to circle his head,
Weave his crown softly now,
No thorn to harm his brow,
Wind it with kisses and small stars instead.

Sue Cowling

The Sky Exploded

Night turned inside out
And suddenly was all ablaze
Across the blue-black sky
Like diamonds. It was day,
Like rainbows sparkling in salt spray,
Or waterfalls of light . . .
Not any sort of night
That anyone had ever seen before
       – or since.
The shepherds on the hill
screwed up their eyes against it
       – so bright it made them wince.
They heard the singing,
felt the wind's wild wings beating,
       – white and gleaming thunder
high in God's heaven.

All this.
All this fanfare-fuss, this mad amazing energy,
On this high hilltop,
This was not the main event.
That happened quietly behind the pub
In a shed they kept the donkey in.

There God was born
Not in a palace to be claimed by kings
Not in a rich man's house awash with *things*.
Not even underneath the angels' shining wings
But in a shed. With stuff.
For us. For ordinary us.

Jan Dean

School is over

School is over.
School is done.
We can stop learning
And start having fun.

Anon.

Hanukkah

Summoning the
 sun
the Hanukkah lamp
 glows
the miracle
 reborn

David Shalem

Light the Festive Candles
(for Hanukkah)

Light the first of eight tonight –
the farthest candle to the right.

Light the first and second too,
when tomorrow's day is through.

Then light three, and then light four –
every dusk one candle more

Till all eight burn bright and high,
honouring a day gone by

When the Temple was restored,
rescued from the Syrian lord,

And an eight-day feast proclaimed –
The Festival of Lights – well named

To celebrate the joyous day
when we regained the right to pray
to our one God in our own way.

Aileen Fisher

Christmas Eve

On Christmas Eve
it is so late
that even Mum and Dad
are fast asleep in bed

I stand at the top of the stairs.

The house is warm
and the tree lights glow

I can smell mince pies
and anticipation

I make a wish.

Roger Stevens

The First Tree in the Greenwood

Now the holly bears a berry as white as the milk,
And Mary bore Jesus, who was wrapped up in silk:
And Mary bore Jesus Christ,
Our Saviour for to be,
And the first tree in the greenwood, it was the holly.

Now the holly bears a berry as green as the grass,
And Mary bore Jesus, who died on the cross:
And Mary bore Jesus Christ,
Our Saviour for to be,
And the first tree in the greenwood, it was the holly.

Now the holly bears a berry as black as the coal,
And Mary bore Jesus, who died for us all:
And Mary bore Jesus Christ,
Our Saviour for to be,
And the first tree in the greenwood, it was the holly.

Now the holly bears a berry, as blood is it red,
Then trust we our Saviour, who rose from the dead:
And Mary bore Jesus Christ,
Our Saviour for to be,
And the first tree in the greenwood, it was the holly.

Anon.

Winter (written aged 10)

Frost curls, ice creeps
Over lake, still and deep.
Bracken's flat, dying red,
Frost's curling overhead.
Twinkling hill tops, flakes of snow,
Starving seagulls swooping low.
Breath frosts, feet stamp.
House warm, world damp.
Toes glow, baths steam,
Santa Claus, reindeer dream.

Christmas trees, cards and bells,
Snow melts, river swells.
Water freezing, skates out,
Roaring fire, gathering about.
Cribs are lit, church bells chime,
Windows glow at Christmas time.
Warm pyjamas, bed snug,
Cuddled up in winter's hug.
Think of mugs of steaming drink,
Santa's sleigh bells chime and chink.
Owls hunt, trees stand bare,
Snow blankets everywhere.
Cosy evenings, frosty days,
Watery sun in misty haze.
Patchwork quilts, polar bears,
Woolly winter and underwear.

Julia Rawlinson

The Lost Pantomime

Where's the pantomime?
It's behind you!
Oh no it isn't!
Oh yes it is!

Nick Toczek

Toboggan

Take me where the snow lies deep
On some hillside high and steep.
Boldly sit astride my sleigh
One good push and I'm away.
Going speeding down the hill.
Getting faster – What a thrill!
At the bottom brush off snow.
Now to the top for another go.

David Whitehead

Putting Away Christmas

The cards sit in a pile – a child,
dressed as a Christmas pudding,
walks along the top.

The tree lies outside –
pointing the way
for a council collection.

The fairy lights are curled up
inside their plastic box,
resting their filaments for another year.

Time to fold gold wrapping into bags,
read instructions on presents,
press my finger

on the last crumbs
of the Christmas cake,
and lick the sweetness away.

Chrissie Gittins

A Poetry Teacher from Limerick

A poetry teacher from Limerick
Was always very confused
Cos nothing much rhymed
With the name of his town
So why name a rhyming verse after it?

Paul Cookson

Almost New Year

It's the last afternoon
of the old year
and already a full fat moon
is in charge of the sky.
It has nudged the sun
into a distant lake
and left it to drown,
while bare branch trees
like blackened fireworks
burst with sunset.
Frost is patterning the fields,
a tractor tries to furrow
the iron hard hill.
Winter's frown settles
on the face of the landscape.
It shrugs its shoulders,
gives in to January.

Brian Moses

Index of First Lines

Index of First Lines

Index of Titles

Index of Titles

Index of Titles

Index of Titles

Index of Titles

Index of Poets

Index of Poets

Acknowledgements

The compiler and publisher wish to thank the following for permission to use copyright material:

Archer, Petonelle, 'Story Time' by permission of the author; **Ardagh, Philip,** 'A Mouthpiece in a Cluster of Air' and 'St Judas Welcomes Author Philip Arder' both by permission of the author; **Bateman, David,** 'French Lessons', 'A Near Miss' and 'A Trip to the Art Gallery' all by permission of the author; **Bates, Susan,** 'Silent Pee' by permission of the author; **Benson, Catherine,** 'Elvin' from *Look Out! The Teachers are Coming!*, Macmillan Children's Books, 2005, by permission of the author; **Benson, Gerard,** 'One More Day' and 'School for Wizards and Witches' from *Omba Balomba: Poems by Gerard Benson*, Smith/Doorstop 2005, 'The Injection' and 'Spring Assembly' from *To Catch an Elephant: Poems by Gerard Benson*, Smith/Doorstop, 2002, and 'Out of Class' all by permission of the author; **Bevan, Clare,** 'The New Girl' from *Spooky Schools*, ed. Brian Moses, Macmillan Children's Books, 'Literacy Hour' from *The Teacher's Revenge*, ed. Brian Moses, Macmillan Children's Books, 'Long Division Lesson' from *One River, Many Creeks*, ed. Valerie Bloom, Macmillan Children's Books, 'The Music Lesson Rap' from *The Rhyme Riot*, ed. Gaby Morgan, Macmillan Children's Books, 'Playground Song' from *Poems for Year Four*, ed. Pie Corbett, Macmillan Children's Books, 'Just Doing My Job', 'A Teacher's Epitaph', 'B is For Books', 'Hi Ho, Hi Ho', and 'L is For Library' all by permission of the author; **Billings, Ian,** 'Beware! Take Care' by permission of the author; **Bonner, Ann,** 'Chinese New Year' from *Scholastic Collections*, ed. Jill Bennett, Scholastic 1994, 'Teachers' Holidays' from *The Top Secret Lives of Teachers*, ed. Brian Moses, Macmillan Children's Books, 'Assembly Haiku' from *The Teacher's Revenge*, ed. Brian Moses, Macmillan Children's Books, 'Netball' and 'Looking Forward to Divali' from *School Poems*, ed. Jennifer Curry, Scholastic 1999, 'The Harvest Queen' from *Let's Celebrate*, ed. John Foster, Oxford University Press, 1989, and 'School Photo Haiku' all by permission of the author; **Bower, Tony,** 'The Size of the Problem' by permission of the author; **Brandling, Redvers,** 'Playtime' by permission of the author; **Bright, Paul**, 'Up in Smoke'and 'Science Stinks' both by permission of the author; **Brownlee, Liz**, 'April 1st' by permission of the author; **Calder, Dave**, 'Assembly', 'The Desk', 'Map', 'Pencil', 'Rules of the Game', 'Changed', 'Drawer', 'Arithmetic', 'Where Is Everybody?', 'Good Morning', and 'The Ascent of Vinicombe' all by permission of the author; **Carter, James**, 'Playground Wanderer' by permission of the author; **Carter, Lisa**, 'What For?' by permission of the author; **Cashdan, Liz**, 'Netball' by permission of the author; **Chatterjee, Debjani**, 'What Book Am I?' from *The Universal Vacuum Cleaner and Other Riddle Poems*, ed. John Foster, Oxford University Press, 2005, 'The Truant's School Report', 'Memories of Schooldays' and 'School Bell Haiku' all by permission of the author; **Chisholm, Alison**, 'Summer Fair' from *The School Year*, ed. Brian Moses, Macmillan Children's Books, 2001, by permission of the author; **Christopher, Donavan**, 'Books R4 Everyone' by permission of the author; **Clarke, Jane**, 'Ice' and 'A Cold's Going Round' both by permission of the author; **Clarke, John**, 'Last Week of Term and He Wants Us to Write', 'The End of the Holidays', 'Melting Pot' and 'Visiting Poet' all by permission of the author; **Coe, Mandy**, 'How the Light/how the Dark', 'The Sunshine of Mandy Browne', 'Me and You', 'Shut Down', 'When Mrs Smith Slammed the Classroom Door', 'Schooldays End', 'The Head's First Name', and 'Thank You' all by permission of the author; **Coelho, Joseph**, 'Make It Bigger, Eileen!', 'Hamster! Hamster!', 'Miss Flotsam', 'Lace Trouble' and 'How to Kill a Poet' all by permission of the author; **Coldwell, John**, 'Thirteen Questions' by permission of the author; **Cookson, Paul**, 'Playtime Footie', 'It's Raining on the Trip', 'Prayer for the First Day of the School Holidays', 'Prayer for the Last Day of the School Holidays', 'These Are the Hands', 'Where Teacher's Keep Their Pets', 'Teacher's Very Quiet Today', 'What Mr Kenning Does When He Thinks We Aren't Looking'and 'A Poetry Teacher from Limerick' all by permission of the author; **Corbett, Pie**, 'If Only'and 'Early Winter Diary Poem' both by permission of the author; **Corti, Doris**, 'Starfish and Other Shapes' from *One in a Million*, Viking, by permission of the author; **Costello-McFeat, Karen**, 'The Weird Dinner Ladies', 'Fellow Suffering' and 'School Survival Kit' all by permission of the author; **Cowling, Sue**, 'Words Behaving Badly' and 'Coronation' both by permission of the author; **Curry, Jennifer**, 'Winter

Acknowledgements

Playground' and 'Not a Nightingale' both by permission of the author; **Dean, Jan,** 'Here Lies Mad Lil' from *The Jumble Book*, ed. Roger Stevens, Macmillan Children's Books, 2009, 'Girl in the Library' from *Nearly Thirteen*, ed. Anne Harvey, Blackie, 1993, 'Fraction', 'Tent' from *Wallpapering the Cat*, Macmillan Children's Books, 2003, 'Colouring In' from *Mice on Ice*, ed. Gaby Morgan, Macmillan Children's Books, 2004, 'Chinese Water Torture', 'It's Not What I'm Used To', 'Their Secret Is Out' from *A Mean Fish Smile*, Macmillan Children's Books, 2000, 'The Sky Exploded' from *Read Me Out Loud!*, eds. Paul Cookson and Nick Toczek, Macmillan Children's Books, 2007, 'Pond Dipping' and 'Turning Over' all by permission of the author; **Denton, Graham,** 'Pupil Troubles'and 'Mum's Umbrage' from *The Jumble Book*, ed. Roger Stevens, Macmillan Children's Books, 2009, 'Misleading Reading' from *The Dog Ate My Bus Pass*, Macmillan Children's Books, 2004, and 'Cinquain' all by permission of the author; **Desmond, John C.,** 'Summer' by permission of the author; **Dixon, Peter,** 'The Colour of My Dreams', 'Awe and Wonder', 'Sticking the Stars', 'School Clubs' and 'The Collector' all by permission of the author; **d'Lacey, Chris,** 'The Great Shove Ha'Penny Craze', 'Tank', 'Drawing Dragons' and 'Speech Day at Mount Augustine's in the Field' all by permission of the author; **Doherty, Berlie,** 'I Hear', 'If You Were a Carrot' from *Walking On Air*, Harper Collins, 1993, and 'Quieter Than Snow' from *Casting a Spell*, Orchard, 1991, all by permission of the author; **Dove, Jill** 'Mr Marks and the Seasons' by permission of the author; **Durant, Alan,** 'Boy at the Somme' by permission of the author; **England, Jane,** 'Bladderwrack' by permission of the author; **Finney, Eric,** Stop Calling Me, Snow' from *Snow Poems*, ed. John Foster, Oxford University Press, 1990, 'Daisies' from *Billy and the Church Hall Sale*, by Eric Finney, Edward Arnold, 1986, 'Dreamer' from *Excuses, Excuses*, ed. John Foster, Oxford University Press, 1997, and 'Cats Rule, OK?' all by permission of the author; **Floyd, Gillian,** 'At Lunchtime', 'Mrs Mackenzie', 'Waiting for the Start of Term' all by permission of the author; **Foster, John,** 'The Schoolkids' Rap', 'Four O'clock Friday', 'Size-wise', 'Writing and Sums', 'Holidays', 'Inside Sir's Matchbox', 'The Bell', 'Hello, Mr Visitor' and 'Teachers!' from *The Poetry Chest*, by John Foster, Oxford University Press, 2007, all by permission of the author; **Gallagher, Katherine,**

Acknowledgements

'Christmas Spirit', from *The Big Book of Christmas*, Macmillan Children's Books, 2005, 'Moonwatch', from *Propisia*, Vol. 1, 2, 2008, 'Bullies' from *Them and Us*, Bodley Head, 1993, and 'At the School Camp' all by permission of the author; **Gittins, Chrissie**, 'The Pencil Stub', 'Limpet' and 'Putting Away Christmas' from *I Don't Want an Avocado for an Uncle*, Rabbit Hole Publications, 2006, and 'Beach for Ruksar' and 'What Does Poetry Do?' from *Now You See Me, Now You...*, Rabbit Hole Publications, 2002, all by permission of the author; **Green, Mary**, 'Forbidden Territory' and 'Miss Fleur' from *When the Teacher Isn't Looking*, Macmillan Children's Books, 2001, both by permission of the author; **Hardy-Dawson, Sue**, 'Poem About the Injustice of Being Made to Stand Outside in the Rain at Playtime'and 'School Holiday Blues' both by permission of the author; **Harmer, David**, 'Winter Morning: Winter Night', 'The Inspector's Report', 'We Lost Our Teacher to the Sea', 'Nearly', 'On a Blue Day', 'Some Days', 'Help!' and 'The Last Laugh' all by permission of the author; **Henderson, Stewart**, 'I take me for granted', first broadcast as part of the BBC Radio series *Wide Awake at Bedtime*, 2008, by permission of the author; **Henry, Paul**, 'After the Fire' by permission of the author; **Hoyer, Monica**, 'Not Only Pebbles' by permission of the author; **Hughes, Paddy**, 'The School Fireworks Show' by permission of the author; **Johnson, Mike**, 'New Year Resolution', 'Amazing Maisie', 'Science Lesson' and 'Tall Story' all by permission of the author; **Joseph, Jenny**, 'Poem for Scowly-face dragging his feet on the way to school' and 'Towards the End of the Summer' both by permission of the author; **Kavanagh, Michael**, 'Potions' and 'Summer at Granny's House' both by permission of the author; **Kitching, John**, 'Miss Spry' by permission of the author; **Knight, Stephen**, 'Late July' from *Sardines and Other Poems*, by Stephen Knight, Young Picador, 2004, by permission of the author; **Langham, Tony**, 'Rainy Monday Morning Playtime Blues' and 'Sir's a Secret Agent' both by permission of the author; **Lawson, JonArno**, 'Underneath the School' and 'In Front of Me' both by permission of the author; **Leighton, Patricia**, 'Easter in School' from *The School Year*, ed. Brian Moses, Macmillan Children's Books, 2001, 'Watching', 'Madcap Days', 'Lunchtime Swaps' and 'The Happy Memories Bench', all by permission of the author; **MacRae, Lindsay**, 'The Interesting Table' from *You Canny Shove Yer Granny Off a Bus!*, Puffin, 1995, by permission of the author; **Magee, Wes,** 'At the End of a School Day'and 'The Super Sledging Stars' both by permission of the author; **Mann, Jane,** 'Special to Me' by permission of the author; **McEwan, Colin,** 'Cold Day – Edinburgh' by permission of the author; **McMillan, Ian,** 'Routes' by permission of the author; **Mellor, Robin,** 'Bug Olympics'and 'The School Band' both by permission of the author; **Millum, Trevor,** 'Photo Opportunity', 'Bell Rings' and 'Holiday Diary' all by permission of the author; **Moses, Brian,** 'How Teachers Leave School Each Evening', 'The School Goalie's Reasons . . .', 'The I-Spy Book of Teachers' from *Taking Out the Tigers*, Poems by Brian Moses, Macmillan Children's Books, 2005, 'Day Closure' from *The Secret Lives of Teachers*, ed. Brian Moses, Macmillan Children's Books, 1996, 'Mrs Smellie' from *The Truth About Teachers*, by James Carter, Brian Moses, Paul Cookson and David Harmer, Macmillan Children's Books, 2007, 'Windy Plaground' from *Knock Down Ginger and Other Poems*, by Brian Moses, Cambridge University Press, 1994, and 'Almost New Year' from *Read Me Out Loud!*, ed. Paul Cookson and Nick Toczek, Macmillan Children's Books, 2007, all by permission of the author; **Nagle, Frances,** 'Changing Time' from *You Can't Call a Hedgehog Hopscotch*, Dagger Press, by permission of the author; **Norman, Tony,** 'The School Yard in the Snow' by permission of the author; **Norton, Maggie,** 'In the School Garden' by permission of the author; **Orme, David,** 'Football in the Rain' by permission of the author; **Owen, Gareth,** 'Dear Examiner', 'Days at School', 'Miss Creedle Teaches Creative Writing' all by permission of the author; **Parelkar, Ruhee,** 'A Poetry on Geometry' by permission of the author; **Parsons, Trevor,** 'Front of the Class', 'Happy Birthday St Michaels', 'The Photograph', 'When Is a Thing a Living Thing?' all by permission of the author; **Patten, Brian,** 'Remembering Snow' from *Juggling with Gerbils*, Puffin, 2000, and 'Geography Lesson' both by permission of the author; **Phinn, Gervase,** 'A Proper Poet' and 'Reading Round the Class' from *It Takes One to Know One* both by permission of the author; **Pitt, Simon,** 'At the End of School Assembly' and 'Trouble Ahead' both by permission of the author; **Poulson, Joan,** 'Dragonships', 'Shorthand', 'Wilderness', 'Last Dive of the Day', 'Words Are Magic', 'Magnify', 'Harvest' and 'Christmas Music' all by permission of the author; **Rawlinson, Julia,** 'A Wonderful Week' from *The Jumble Book*, ed. Roger

Stevens, Macmillan Children's Books, 2009, 'Timetable' from *Spooky Schools*, ed. Brian Moses, Macmillan Children's Books, 2004, and 'Winter' from *The Big Book of Christmas*, ed. Gaby Morgan, Macmillan Children's Books, 2005, all by permission of the author; **Rawnsley, Irene**, 'Flying' and 'Painting' from *Ask a Silly Question* by Irene Rawnsley, Methuen, 1988, and 'Good Girls' from *The House of a Hundred Cats* by Irene Rawnsley; Methuen, 1995, all by permission of the author; **Rice, John**, 'School Crime' from *School Poems*, ed. Susie Gibbs, Oxford University Press, 2001, 'The Romans' from *Guzzling Jelly with Giant Gorbelly* by John Rice, Macmillan Children's Books, 2004, 'Going to Secondary' from *The School Year*, ed. Brian Moses, Macmillan Children's Books, 2001, 'Mr Body, Our Head' from *Zoomballoomballistic* by John Rice, Aten Press, 1981, and 'The Ghosts of the Children Who Attended This School Before Us' and 'The Fairy School Under the Loch' all by permission of the author; **Rumble, Coral**, 'Sum Haiku' from *Poetry Forms*, ed. David Harmer, Folens, 1999, by permission of the author; **Sail, Lawrence**, 'Out of Hours' and '29th February' both by permission of the author; **Scannell, Vernon**, 'Moving House' by permission of the Literary Estate of the author; **Sedgwick, Fred**, 'Girl with a Worksheet in a Castle' and 'On the First Day of the Summer Holidays' both by permission of the author; **Sensier, Danielle**, 'Experiment', 'Headmistress', 'And the Ball Hums', 'It's Only a Matter of Time' all by permission of the author; **Shavick, Andrea**, 'Batgirl's Disgrace' by permission of the author; **Simpson, Matt**, 'Grandad's Garden' from *What the Wind Said! A Collection of Poems for Children* by Matt Simpson, Greenwich Exchange, 2008, by permission of the author; **Smith, Sue**, 'Do Your Own Thing', 'Sports Day' and 'Teacher Next Door!' all by permission of the author; **Stevens, Roger**, 'Mr Walton's on the Playground' and 'The Estuary Field Trip' from *I Did Not Eat the Goldfish*, Macmillan Children's Books, 2002, 'Who Lives in the School Pond?', 'Silent Song', 'Helen's Lunch Box', 'Billy's Lunch Box', 'What We Did on Our Holidays', 'Frog Class', 'The Football Team', 'Nature Table', 'Poems Don't Have to Rhyme' and 'Where Do Poems Come From?' all from *On My Way to School I Saw a Dinosaur*, Hands Up Books, 2005, and 'Teacher's Pet' all by permission of the author; **Stewart, Pauline**, 'New Boy' by permission of the author; **Swinger, Marian**, 'The Escape', 'The School Nature Table', 'Green School',

Acknowledgements

'Late Again', 'A Multiplication of One' and 'The Walking Bus' all by permission of the author; **Thom, Marie,** 'The Playground' and 'School' both by permission of the author; **Toczek, Nick,** 'Staff Meeting' and 'The Lost Pantomine' both by permission of the author; **Topping, Angela,** 'It's True' and 'The Staff' from *Teachers' Pets*, ed. Paul Cookson, Macmillan Children's Books, 1999, 'Our Headmaster', 'End of Term Reports', 'Four O'clock Snack', 'Our Claire', and 'The Imaginative Schoolchild' all by permission of the author; **Townsend, Jill,** 'Roman Day', 'Who's Here?', 'Rumour', 'Visiting the Castle' and 'Holidays: Day 3' all by permission of the author; **Turner, Steve,** 'Assembly', 'Girls and Boys Come Out to Play' and 'Questions' all from *The Moon Has Got My Pants On*, Lion, 2001, 'Why Are You Late for School?' from *Dad, You're Not Funny*, Lion, 1999, and 'Careers Advice' from *I Was Only Asking*, Lion, 2004, all by permission of the author; **Underhill, Ruth,** 'The School Bag' and 'After School Club' both by permission of the author; **Waddell, Philip,** 'No Feel For Numbers' and 'An Average Poem' both by permission of the author; **Wade, Barry,** 'Tadpoles' by permission of the author; **Ward, Dave,** 'The Last Boy in School' and 'After School' both by permission of the author; **Warren, Celia,** 'The Soggy End of Science' and 'When Every Teacher Knows Your Name' both by permission of the author; **Welch, Linda Lee,** 'Family', 'I Am Full of Promise', 'Schooldays' and 'Wants and Needs' all by permission of the author; **Whitehead, David,** 'Squirrels and Motorbikes' from *The School Year*, ed. Brian Moses, Macmillan Children's Books, 2001, and 'Toboggan' from *Secrets*, ed. Judith Nicholls, Ginn, both by permission of the author; **Whittingham, Brian,** 'Catch a Rainbow', 'Dress Sense' and 'Mister Nobody' from *Septimus Pitt and the Grumbleoids*, Luath Press, all by permission of the author; **Williams, Kate,** 'The Trees Behind the Teachers' Cars: Autumn Term', 'The Trees Behind the Teachers' Cars: First Day Back', 'The Trees Behind the Teachers' Cars: Spring Term', 'The Trees Behind the Teachers' Cars: Summer Term' and 'School Trip Trauma' all by permission of the author; **Young, Bernard,** 'Every Night Mr Miller Dreams' from *Wanted Alive*, Hands Up Books, 2004, 'Absent' from *Brilliant!*, Kingston Press, 2000, and 'Easy Does It' all by permission of the author.

Every effort has been made to trace the copyright holders, but if any have been inadvertently overlooked the publishers will be pleased to make the necessary arrangement at the first opportunity.

A selected list of titles available from Macmillan Children's Books

The prices shown below are correct at the time of going to press. However, Macmillan Publishers reserves the right to show new retail prices on covers, which may differ from those previously advertised.

Read Me 1	978-0-330-37353-1	£6.99
Read Me 2	978-0-330-39132-0	£6.99
Read Me and Laugh	978-0-330-43557-4	£6.99
Read Me Out Loud!	978-0-330-44621-1	£6.99
The Works	978-0-330-48104-5	£6.99
The Works 2	978-0-330-39902-9	£6.99
The Works 3	978-0-330-41578-1	£6.99
The Works 4	978-0-330-43644-1	£6.99
The Works 5	978-0-330-39870-1	£5.99
The Works 6	978-0-330-43439-3	£6.99
The Works 7	978-0-330-44424-8	£6.99
The Works 8	978-0-330-46407-9	£7.99
The Works Key Stage 1	978-0-330-43947-3	£5.99
The Works Key Stage 2	978-0-330-43949-7	£5.99

All Pan Macmillan titles can be ordered from our website, www.panmacmillan.com, or from your local bookshop and are also available by post from:

Bookpost, PO Box 29, Douglas, Isle of Man IM99 1BQ
Credit cards accepted. For details:
Telephone: 01624 677237
Fax: 01624 670923
Email: bookshop@enterprise.net
www.bookpost.co.uk

Free postage and packing in the United Kingdom